Quilts

THE FABRIC OF FRIENDSHIP

THE YORK COUNTY QUILT DOCUMENTATION PROJECT AND THE YORK COUNTY HERITAGE TRUST

BOOK COMMITTEE: SHARON P. ANGELO, CAROL C. BLEVINS,
BARBARA A. GARRETT, JOAN U. HAMME, DAWN HEEFNER, POLLY STETLER

Schiffer Publishing Ltd

4880 Lower Valley Road, Atglen, PA 19310 USA

Dedication

This book is dedicated to the quiltmakers of the past, in whom we all recognize a bit of ourselves.

Library of Congress Cataloging-in-Publication Data

Quilts: the fabric of friendship / the York County Quilt Documentation Project and the York County Heritage Trust Book Committee, Sharon P. Angelo...[et al.].
p. cm.
ISBN 0-7643-1195-6 (pbk.)
1. Quilts--Pennsylvania--York County--History--19th century. 2. Quilts--Pennsylvania--York County--History--20th century. I. Angelo, Sharon P. II. York County Quilt Documentation Project (York County, Pa.) III. York County Heritage Trust (York County, Pa.). Book Committee.
NK9112.Q59 2000
746.46'09748'41--dc21
00-009620

Designed by Bonnie M. Hensley
Type set in Zapf Humanist 601 BT/Humanist 521 BT

ISBN: 0-7643-1195-6
Printed in China
1 2 3 4

Published by Schiffer Publishing Ltd.
4880 Lower Valley Road
Atglen, PA 19310
Phone: (610) 593-1777; Fax: (610) 593-2002
E-mail: Schifferbk@aol.com
Please visit our web site catalog at **www.schifferbooks.com**
We are always looking for people to write books on new and related subjects. If you have an idea for a book, please contact us at the above address.

This book may be purchased from the publisher.
Include $3.95 for shipping.
Please try your bookstore first.
You may write for a free catalog.

In Europe, Schiffer books are distributed by
Bushwood Books
6 Marksbury Ave.
Kew Gardens
Surrey TW9 4JF England
Phone: 44 (0) 20 8392-8585
Fax: 44 (0) 20 8392-9876
E-mail: Bushwd@aol.com
Free postage in the UK. Europe: air mail at cost.

Contents

Acknowledgments

The Project Committee wishes to thank the multitude of individuals and organizations who made the York County Quilt Documentation a success. Let's start with the honored quiltmakers of yesteryear—and their descendants who graciously brought their quilts to us for documentation. You have our utmost appreciation. While not all the documented quilts could be included in this book, they all have earned an honored place in the heritage of York County.

We would like to thank the following sites for kindly welcoming our teams to their facility for a Discovery Day (our name for the events where the public was invited to bring in their quilts for documentation). Listed next to each site is the respective site captain. They each hold a special place in the world of quilt documentation.

Bethlehem Stonepile United Methodist Church, Red Lion — Carol Blevins
Red Land Community Library, Etters — Mary Gail Conley
St. Paul Lutheran Church, Hametown — Ann Biser-Rohrbaugh
Hanover YWCA, Hanover — Bobbe Benvin
Pine Grove Presbyterian Church, Airville — Rosemarie Smith
Wellsville Fire Hall, Wellsville — Judy Deveney
Trinity United Church of Christ, Hellam — Wendy Buchart
Saint Paul Lutheran Church, York — Cindy Martin
Failor's Photography Studio, Red Lion — The Committee
The York County Heritage Trust, York — The Committee
First Church of the Brethren, East York — Jutta Creager

Luther Memorial Evangelical Lutheran Church, York — The Committee
Union Lutheran Church, York — Rachael Tracey

Our on-site quilt consultants provided the much-needed expertise and experience of dating antique quilts and fabrics. Thank you to Barbara Garrett, Dawn Heefner, and Nancy Roan.

Financial support for this book, the Documentation Project, and the exhibit at The York County Heritage Trust (November 10, 2000 - March 31, 2001) came from many sources. All of our donors took a significant leap of faith on our behalf, and we are most grateful for their belief in the worthiness of the project — and in us. First and foremost, we thank the Robert P. Turner Publication Fund of The York County Heritage Trust for contributing to the publication of this book. The support of this fund and that of the Publications Committee of the Trust were essential to this work, and we are most grateful for their commitment to preserving York County history. We are indebted to the financial support from the following: The Auxiliary of The York County Heritage Trust, York Federal Savings and Loan, Mr. and Mrs. Thomas W. Wolf, The York Quilters' Guild, The Quilter's Guild of Dallas, Mr. and Mrs. James Chinault, numerous in-kind contributions from Susquehanna Pfaltzgraff Co., the York County Association of Family and Consumer Sciences, and a special few who chose to remain anonymous. The York County 250th Anniversary Commission was a tremendous help throughout the project, by way of publicity and sponsorship of the 250th Commemorative Quilt. The lack of turned-in receipts by committee members and the overflowing donation box on the exit table at each of our Discovery Days have not gone unnoticed. The fund-raising signature quilt brought an additional $2,284, thanks to Carol Blevins, her sewing team, and the generous folks of York County who supported the project with their signature.

Thank you to our Publicity Committee for getting the word out, far and near. Due to the hard work of the committee, along with the media's response, we shared the joy of busy Discovery Days.

Photography help came from many directions. Our amateur team from the York Quilters' Guild became quite professional before it was over. Thank you, Rachael Tracey and Jutta Creager. Professional photographers Scott and Ruthie Failor from Failor's Studio in Red Lion surprised us by donating the two days that we needed them. Unexpected generosity of that nature is truly exceptional.

Now...the ladies! A big heartfelt thank you and group hug to the hard-working crew of volunteers that made the Documentation a success:

Sheila Arnold, Ellie Bennett, Bobbe Benvin, Erika Bergmann, Ann Biser-Rohrbaugh, Lana Blevins, Sara Born, Betty Bortner, Diane Brown, Wendy Buchart, Katie Christopher, Joan Clippinger, Barbara Colvin, Sandy Comer, Mary Gail Conley, Gloria Cooksey, Jutta Creager, Sylvia Crone, Faye Decker, Judy Deveney, Marion Dravk, Carolyn Garner, Ruth Ann Hallman, Patsy Hartnett, Nancy Hershner, Azalea Hinkle, Mary Gertrude Kirsch, Joan Lamberson, Doris Leas, Ginny Lehr, Shirley Leister, Bonnie Lenkner, Audrey Markel, Cindy Martin, Elizabeth Morrison, Pat Mroziak, Phyllis Nelson, Linda Nixon, Pat Oden, Patti Owens, Pat Peña, Louise Pfefferle, Lynn Phillips, Erma Raver, Linda Rohrbaugh, Velma Rosenberg, Jean Roser, Marion Sachs, Diane Salisbury, Carol Lee Shirk, Eileen Shrey, Carol Small, Dawn Small, Linda Smith, Rosemarie Smith, Nancy Spiese, Sue Stauffer, Emmy Lee Steigelman, Leona Stump, Dorothy Taylor, Marilyn Tenenoff, Anita Tickle, Rachael Tracey, Phyllis Twigg, Martha Van Order, Mary Faith Van Noy, Jill Volz, Fernglen Wiherle, Shelley Blevins Wilson, Daisy Wilt, Barbara Wilke, Lauren Wilke, and Hazel Wood.

The Documentation project and the book would not have been possible without the support of our co-sponsor, The York County Heritage Trust. Thank you, in particular, to the following: Janet Deranian, Lila Fourhman-Shaull, Rudolph Hershey, Fran Herzog, Ruth Ann Hirschman, Dennis Kunkle, Justine Landis, June Lloyd, Lamar Matthew, Gayle Petty-Johnson, Donna Schiding, and Heather Taylor. Thanks, too, to Patrick Foltz, now of Preservation Pennsylvania.

The book was a project unto itself. Dawn Heefner gave freely of her time and knowledge, and her writing abilities are matched only by her passion for quilting and history. Without her help this book would not have happened. Our appreciation also goes to Barbara Garrett for her contributions to the writing of the text, to Lamar Matthew and Frances Wolf for their insights on York County and memory in quilting, respectively, and to Cindy Martin for her research abilities. Thanks also to Sheila Painter, Corinne Arugunes, Colleen Burkett, Connie Frye, Lavonne Miller, Pat Smith, and Bill Ward, and the kind people at Schiffer Publishing for their invaluable assistance. Our deepest gratitude to you all.

Finally, the Documentation and this book have consumed hours and hours away from our friends and families. We are grateful for their sacrifice and support. And guess what? We're coming home!

The Project Committee for the Quilt Documentation:

Judy Anderson, Sharon Angelo, Carol Blevins, Janet Chinault, Ann Fetterman, Joan Hamme, Betsey Nyeste, and Polly Stetler.

YORK COUNTY
1998
1999
QUILT
DOCUMENTATION
PROJECT

A Note to the Reader

The poem excerpts at the beginning of each chapter and at the closing are from "The Quilting," written by H.L. Fisher, of York, Pennsylvania, in 1888. The poem in its entirety was originally printed in *Olden Times, or Pennsylvania Rural Life, Some Fifty Years Ago, and Other Poems*, York, Pennsylvania, Fisher Bros., Publishers.

In general, this book is divided into categories that represent the major quilt types, such as appliqué, pieced, and so on. Each chapter contains examples of the various quilt types plus small family vignettes, then concludes with a more expanded York County family history that relates to the chapter. The family information contained in this book has been provided through oral histories taken during the Quilt Documentation process. Every attempt has been made to verify their accuracy, but the very nature of oral histories makes them somewhat elusive.

Quilt pattern names can vary by time period, geographical region, and even by family. Where possible, the quilts within this book are referred to by the most commonly used name.

Yo-Yo, c. 1930, pieced cotton, by Elizabeth Henrietta Hamme, West York, 104" x 89". *Collection of Joan U. Hamme.*

Women, Friendship, and Quilts

by Joan U. Hamme, Chairman, The York County Quilt Documentation Project

Traditionally, quilts have been a creative outlet for formerly voiceless women. The committee for the York County Quilt Documentation Project, with the help and support of the York Quilters' Guild, The York County Heritage Trust, and the York community, heard and responded to those voices. We made a collective commitment to the community, to future scholars, and to quilt collectors to discover York County's quilts and their stories and to record them for all time. This book is the result of our work, and the project committee is proud to add the beauty, art, and spirit of our quilts to the historical legacy of our home.

Other states and Pennsylvania counties have held quilt documentations that have uncovered valuable regional history and lifestyles of early American women. A quilt is a reflection of an era, mirroring a quiltmaker's feelings and political beliefs through her quiet creativity. A quilt documentation is a count, a statistical analysis, a history lesson in fabrics, thread, design, and color. When the quilt meets the quilt documentation process, our history is connected to our present.

Soon after I accepted the challenge and opportunity to chair the York County Quilt Documentation Project, I heard noted quilt historian Barbara Brackman tell about one of America's first friendship quilts, made by three quilters in Philadelphia in 1761, and signed, "in testimony to our friendship." I realized at that moment that quilt history went much deeper than surface documentation. The bond between a quilt and its makers seemed to be the root of all we were doing, including, most especially, the unspoken link of friendship that bound our volunteers to the women of long ago whose quilts we were going to record.

Like all friendships, this one was demanding. The planning committee worked for a year prior to the "kickoff" in June 1998. We secured sites, organized our teams, structured our dates, raised funds, and spread the word. Our goals were not only to examine, register, and record information for future generations, but also to educate the present generation on the care, conservation, and restoration of these fragile pieces of our past. The volunteers were asked to give their time, their energies, and their Saturdays. With the spirit of our quilting ancestors a primary focus, each volunteer gave her all "in testimony to our friendship."

York County and Its Quilts

York County extends over a large geographic area. To completely cover the county and to encourage quilt owners from all of its parts, sites were planned for the north, south, east, and west, with a few in between. The original plan was to have ten sites within a ten-month period. The Project began with anticipation and expectations, but no certainties. Each Discovery Day would hold its own mystery. We believed and hoped that there would be beautiful antique quilts hidden away that would be brought forth to be shared and documented.

Then they came — each Discovery Day unique from the other. Each one to be appreciated on its own. Each one had its own special beauty and its own special story. AND, they brought quilts! Quilts in plastic bags, quilts in pillowcases, quilts in trunks, quilts in shopping boxes, and quilts in their arms.

We got quilts — nearly 1600 quilts! Far more than we expected, with each site seeming to attract more than the one before. Phone calls came from people who could not make it to Discovery Days, but wanted their quilts documented nonetheless. A small team was chosen to make home visits, and three more sites were added to the schedule.

York County quilts were brought to project sites from Maryland, Massachusetts, Texas, and the Pocono Mountains. Quilt collectors from the American Quilt Study Group made certain that we received completed forms and a picture of their York County quilt from their personal collections. California, Iowa, Virginia, and Maryland are represented in this group. Many museums across America house York County quilts, as near as Harrisburg, Pennsylvania, and as far away as Los Angeles, California. The Shelburne Museum in Shelburne, Vermont, displays the twin quilt to our York County Heritage Trust's recent acquisition, an 1851 album quilt.

Presently there are three old York County quilts in my personal possession. I bring this up due to the way I acquired them. Two were from totally unrelated garage sales two years apart. In each case the quilts were not for sale, but rather, they were laying on the ground covered with second-hand treasures. One was upside down so that the beautiful eight-pointed stars would not interfere with showcasing the items for sale. Each time I bartered for these quilts and each time they went home with me. My third York County quilt is a family treasure. Formerly unknown to me, it was pulled from my in-laws' cedar closet as an offering for a display at the York Quilters' Guild show for the Documentation kickoff. A yo-yo quilt made in 1933 by my mother-in-law, Elizabeth Henrietta Hamme, and since given to me, it stands as yet one more thread of friendship and family.

Discovering Our Past

At each Discovery Day, anticipation buzzed in the busy, crowded room. Activity was everywhere. Quilts were piled at every available spot. The "paperwork marathon" began at the registration table where owner information was taken and a numbered cotton twill tag was pinned to each quilt. Each tag was stamped with the Documentation logo and inscribed with a coded identification number. The next stop was the history-gathering table, where volunteers extracted all available knowledge about the quiltmaker. Each quilt then went to a documentation table, where quilt interest turned to quilt obsession. How much can one know about a quilt? With a magnifying glass and measuring tape, gloved volunteers pored over these treasures with expertise. A scribe with a pencil and a ten-page form was nearby to record the information.

The fun continued at the photography section. An ingenious collapsible frame was constructed for the purpose of photographing delicate quilts of all sizes. Made from wood, the frame measured ninety-six inches by ninety-six inches, and when taken apart, it could fit in the back of a 1992 Honda Accord for transport. When in use, the quilt would lay flat on the frame's surface, then the frame would be flipped to stand at a ninety degree angle — perfect for displaying and photographing quilts. This sight was breathtaking. Even the most ordinary quilt sparkled in this limelight. Photographs were taken of the full-size quilt, as well as close-ups of fabrics, signatures, quilting techniques, backs, and borders. While their quilts made the rounds, the quilt owners would gather by the photo station to wait and watch. All day long, one could hear snippets of conversation: "Could mine be the prettiest?" "Could mine be the oldest? Surely it has the best workmanship." "Look at that one on the frame; it looks brand new. Could it be an old quilt?" "Will I ever get out of here? Oh, what does it matter? Look at these beautiful quilts."

With smiles on their faces and their quilts in tow, quiltmakers and owners finally reached the exit table. Here they were given a certificate of participation, a thank-you note, and information on the care and conservation of their quilts. Many would express not only their gratitude, but also their enjoyment of the day, in spite of a significant and usually unplanned wait.

The doors closed at 3:00 p.m., allowing the volunteers the time needed to finish up paperwork, take down the frame and tables, sweep the floor, pack up the supplies and records, and leave by 5:00, or 5:30, or okay, sometimes 6:00. We were exhausted but exhilarated. Our enthusiasm delayed our departures since, of course, we needed to talk about the exciting "finds" of the day in the parking lot.

Each Site Tells a Story

Warm and touching stories evolved at each of our Discovery Days. We were not only documenting quilts, we were extending our friendships and letting many voices enter this conversation.

Spirited goodwill served as a basis from our start in Red Lion. The *York Daily Record* supported the project with an excellent article complete with full-color photographs of old quilts, as did so many other media sources throughout the project. The enthusiasm mounted for us and the community. We were poised and ready to begin using our new documenting skills. All we needed were quilts. They came, we saw, we documented.

In Etters, our second site, we learned the literal meaning of documenting, when a beautiful signature quilt made by The Ladies Aid Society in Goldsboro was brought in. All of the volunteers gathered with magnifying glasses around this exceptional quilt. It was white on white, featuring white embroidered flowers with white embroidered names inside each white petal. There were at least five hundred white signatures to decipher and record! Documenters struggled long and hard to copy each and every name — the ultimate in a documenting experience.

Likewise, when our team arrived at Hametown on a Friday night to set up, we realized our frame did not fit in the same room as the rest of the documenting activity. So we set it up on the second floor. The workers missed being able to see quilts on the frame, but this was a record day with 136 quilts documented. On that day we all learned to adapt on short notice, as quilts and quilt owners far outnumbered our work force.

We found, and reveled in, our oldest quilt, at the Hanover site, a 1790 palampore. Excitement built as the documenting team also discovered a Lone Star quilt inside a Mariner's Compass quilt. Hints that this was more than an ordinary "quilt within a quilt" became evident since each design had been quilted individually, but its true construction was only confirmed when we held the quilt up to a window and let the light shine through. At Hanover we also saw United States Army fabric for the first time, and appliquéd butterflies were everywhere! Once I looked up and saw four different butterfly designs being documented at one time. But, the star of the show was a quiltmaker of long ago who brought her own high school graduation quilt, one she had helped her grandmother to embroider.

The majesty of nature and the helping hand of friendship highlighted the Airville site in January. This day Mother Nature won first place in beauty and design with an ice storm, and we debated whether to cancel because of travel dangers. However, we braved the weather — and so did the spirited quilt owners of York County. The parking lot was a sheet of ice, so the site captain and her family spent the morning with a pick and a shovel, in testimony to friendship, to make the parking lot safe for all who came. And hardy York Countians did not hesitate to bring their exceptional quilts.

In Airville, many were album quilts that reflect the influence of our Maryland neighbors to the south. One intricately appliquéd beauty was stitched for a weary soldier returning from the Civil War.

In addition to the quilts, another heartwarming story came out of this icy day. One of our loyal volunteers was fourteen-year-old Lauren Wilke. Lauren worked as a scribe as her mother and aunt worked at the documentation table. At this site, she saw for the first time, a "Dancing Daffodil" quilt, a pattern printed on the Mountain Mist batting wrappers in the 1930s. "That's it," she exclaimed, to her aunt and her mother. "That is the quilt I

want for my wedding." Aunt Hazel wasted no time, and this striking quilt is being reproduced for Lauren's hope chest.

The quilt/friendship link continued. One cold morning at the Wellsville Fire Hall, as our gathering was getting started, the sweetest little lady came to me and said, "Is this going to be a great day or what?" and gave me a big hug. And it *was* a great day. We saw everything from quilts inside of quilts, to 1860 crib quilts, to individual quilt blocks. One lady came with her car trunk full of quilts. Vitality was in the room, generated by quilts, smiles, and community spirit.

Our eastern site at the Trinity United Church of Christ in Hellam demonstrated that when quilts and friendship unite, obstacles can be overcome, even out of chaos. At first, it didn't concern me that we were short-handed that day. After all, it was mid-winter and surely most people would come to another site in more predictable weather. Not so. By 10:00 a.m. we had documented seventy-five quilts. People and their quilts filled every available space in the room. They were up the stairs and nearly out the door. The only thing that did not multiply was the number of volunteers. Our schedule of other sites was passed out to those carrying bags full of quilts to encourage them to come another time. Even turning people away, we documented 154 quilts, many of which were previously unseen original designs.

A family story added an important chapter at our site in West York where we had an ideal setting in the fellowship room at Saint Paul Lutheran Church. We took advantage of a large room to display a traveling exhibit from Keepsake Quilting, a program scheduled by the York Quilters' Guild for National Quilt Day. But the absolute highlight of this day was another example of links over time. At this site there was an unplanned uniting of long-lost relatives who recognized each other by the quilts that they brought. Each of them had a quilt made by the same quiltmaker, a common ancestor of theirs who was skilled in original appliqué design.

One's personal life gets woven into this ongoing testimony of friendship. Prior to the second Discovery Day in Red Lion, I flew in at the wee hour of 3:00 a.m., barely allowing enough time to get to the site. I had had a wonderfully exciting weekend attending my son's graduation, and other volunteers allowed me a late arrival. Again, we believed we would see a reduced number of quilts due to competition from the popular Lancaster quilt show, the Easter weekend, and the fact we had been in Red Lion before. Not only did we have a record number of 178 quilts documented that day, but, unknown to me, my husband's aunt and uncle came, bringing a quilt that his uncle had helped his grandmother cut the pieces for.

Friday, May 30, the day before we opened the documentation site to the public at the downtown Historical Society Museum, we were given the opportunity to document the quilts of the museum collection. Since it was a two-day event, my house became the "Documentation Bed & Breakfast." We wanted the expert quilt daters and consultants extraordinaire to be close by for both days. The quilts we saw that day just took our breath away. Anticipation built as each muslin-wrapped quilt was unrolled. Everything literally stopped when the long-awaited John Hewson panel quilt, unrivaled in any antique quilt collection, was unrolled for us to document.

The next day had the appearance of another museum collection day. But, no, these exquisite quilts were brought in from the private collections of the York County people who owned them. This occasion brought the greatest number to date with a total of 197. This was to be our last Discovery Day, our last site, our wrap-up, or so we thought.

But the quilt calls kept coming in. With a tired crew, anxious to have Saturdays back in their lives, we kept going. We did not want to miss anything, so another site was added. We did not advertise; we only wanted the quilts we had missed. With that, another 124 outstanding and unusual beauties were added to the growing collection.

If only that had taken care of everyone, we might have stopped. In November of 1999, the York Quilters' Guild planned an "In Service Day" at their regular meeting, which became our final Discovery Day. We deemed it our "N" site, appropriately situated in our alphabet numbering system, but I believed it stood for "No More."

My Testimony to Quilts

My personal interest in quiltmaking began in 1991 when I needed to make some lifestyle changes due to health issues. My sister in Connecticut knew everything about quilting because she had taken one class. She thought it worthwhile for me to give it a try since I needed something to occupy my time while I remained quiet. She became my quilt coach and when I hit a snag, I would call her long distance to talk me through it. Within a year, I had my twelve scrap blocks pieced and hand quilted, and stock in AT&T. My cardboard template was a little rough around the edges, but I was feeling better.

The handwork was therapeutic as my mind often went to poetic romantic places as I correlated the fabric pieces with remnants of my life. Some blocks were prettier than others, some more expertly done. There were those of which I was very proud and some I felt I should throw in the trash. But they were all there and all effective, one to the other. Put together they looked pretty good, complete and whole, like I wanted to be one day soon. I loved working with my favorite colors but quickly learned that accepting some I didn't like as much certainly added depth and interest to my quilt. I was never mechanical so it took a long time for my machine and me to come to terms. The bobbin was controlling *my* tension instead of me controlling *its* tension. You see I had a lot to learn about machine piecing. Hand quilting also, since I didn't realize that hand stitches were supposed to be little. They were even, they held the quilt together, and they made a lovely design. I wanted to be done now, but the border and binding seemed out of my league. It was — so my sister came to the rescue by visiting to help guide me through it. The first step, she said, was to get rid of those plants and the knick-knacks crowding my workspace. Once I got the idea, she went back to Connecticut and I went to work, determined to finish my quilt. I did finish that quilt.

Finishing that quilt enabled me to focus my attention. I learned to audition fabrics and complement blocks. A viewboard helped me with placement. I looked and I listened and I learned. Two years and two quilts later, urged by a friend I met at a fabric shop, I joined the York Quilters' Guild. I continued to look and to listen and to learn. Quilts — their making, their history and their stories — became an integral part of my life. Yet, my recent life as a quilt researcher has taken me to new places and introduced me to very knowledgeable people in this quilt world. These experiences and all I have learned through them are my rewards. New doors have been put in front of me and I have not hesitated to open them. I continue to look and to listen. Now I invite you, the reader, to enjoy this history of York County, to see its quilts, and to share all that we have learned from the quilts and the stories of those voiceless women of long ago — *in testimony to our friendship*.

A Brief Overview of York County and Its People

by Lamar Matthew, Senior Director of Museum Services, The York County Heritage Trust

York County's history as a place to call home began long before it was neatly defined by borders. For countless millennia native people hunted its thick hardwood forests and fished its network of streams. Waves of migration moved north and south on the great river that is now the county's eastern edge. Some stopped for a time to settle on the river's fertile bottomland where they built villages. Well-established paths crossed east and west and provided trading routes linking these early people with other cultures. Their world changed forever in the late seventeenth century when waves of European immigration touched its shore.

In 1681, King Charles II of England granted a large tract of land west of the Delaware River to his subject William Penn. This land, which was to become known as Pennsylvania, lay south of the New York colony and north of Lord Baltimore's Maryland colony. Penn, unlike any other colonial proprietor, made treaties and purchased this new colony from its native people.

Penn, a dissident Quaker often at odds with the established church, opened his province to all those who sought a place to live and flourish in religious freedom. The first of these people landed on the banks of the Delaware in the 1680s. They came mainly from England, Ireland, Switzerland, and various German principalities. Most of them, like Penn, were dissenting Protestants seeking safe haven. The industrious newcomers cleared vast acreage for farms, laid out roads, and established communities. Soon all the land between Pennsylvania's eastern rivers was parceled out, but still ships arrived daily carrying hopeful immigrants. Expansion beyond the broad Susquehanna River was inevitable.

Subsequent treaties in the 1720s secured all the lands west of the Susquehanna for settlement. Ferries were established at several points on the river and carried settlers and supplies west to open land. As some of the immigrants sought out suitable land, they found large tracts already claimed by settlers pushing north from the Maryland colony. Soon conflicts over property ownership arose in Penn's peaceful province. This struggle was resolved decades later by the historic survey made by Mason and Dixon. Their "line" would become forever known as the point where North meets South.

Three distinct groups took up lands during York County's earliest settlement. They settled in separate parts of the county where they could keep close to their own language, religion, and cultural practices. They brought with them a wealth of customs to impose on the new landscape.

English Quakers from Pennsylvania's crowded eastern counties streamed into the northern reaches of the new territory. They settled into the fertile Redland Valley north of the Conewago Creek. Soon Quakers from the north of Ireland joined them. The culture of simplicity that was part of their faith is still evident in the meetinghouses and farmsteads that they built. The once strong Quaker presence all but vanished in the mid-nineteenth century when many of their numbers moved west.

Scots-Irish Presbyterians crossed the Susquehanna and settled in the southeastern sector of the county. The land they claimed was hilly and cut deep with hollows and steep-sided valleys. As they cleared fields and planted crops they found that the shaley soil of the region needed much improvement. Their determination turned marginal land into productive farms. Villages with lyrical names like Sunnyburn and Castle Finn reveal their founders' roots.

German Protestants, mainly Lutheran, Reformed, and Brethren folk, poured into the central and southwest valleys. Disembarking from ships that arrived daily in the port of Philadelphia, they traveled directly overland to York County. Their land grants in the limestone valleys were naturally fertile and they prospered from their labor. The Germans, above all other founding groups, left noticeable traces of their culture in the region's architecture, farming practices, food, and speech.

Immigration into York County, for the most part, was over by the time of the Revolutionary War. Ethnic populations grew and expanded beyond their original boundaries. Roads crisscrossed the county, linking once iso-lated settlements. Subsequent generations moved beyond those closed communities of their ancestors and began interrelating and intermarrying with others of different heritages. By the mid-nineteenth century the characteristic differences brought by the early settlers began to fade. Germanic overtones diffused throughout the county and entered every aspect of life. By all outward appearances, York County became a "Pennsylvania Dutch" community.

York County has drawn from within and without to form its own styles and culture. A rich heritage coupled with an open eye on life beyond its borders has made York County a part of, rather than apart from, the world. No matter if you are a descendant of an early immigrant or a new arrival to the area, you will find that York County is a great place to call home.

The Quilt as a Site for Memory

by Frances D. Wolf, B.A., M.A.

Slips of fabrics, some of a single color, others patterned by several colors, pieced together to encase a layer of soft substance. In simplest terms, this describes a quilt. But this modest piece of bedding is more complex than that. The quilt's construction from those unassuming remnants of the everyday belies its deeply rich legacy. Through the visual spectacle of its color combinations and abstract geometric designs, as well as its appliquéd organic shapes reminiscent of nature's own, the quilt shows off traditional design motifs. The quilt also represents a craft history through the fineness and complexity of its stitches. It also reminds us of a social history where women came together to sew for one another. Reproduced in paintings and prints, vintage newspapers, periodicals and photos, as well as diaries and letters, the quilt is a quiet but dramatic reminder of a history of women's work, a work that displays the level of their passion and commitment for artistic expression, for fine craft and, most importantly, for community.

The quilter draws upon this rich legacy of traditions as a critical and necessary resource for her own creative work. But the quilter does more than honor this past. Implicit in the act of passing patterns from one quilter to another, across geographic boundaries and through generations, by written sources as well as by word of mouth, is the fact that the quilter remembers. She remembers through her eyes and her hands. She remembers by repeating earlier color combinations and designs in her own work. She remembers by following the same stitching patterns of previous quilt examples. The quilter remembers by each slip of fabric she pieces together and by each stitch she pulls through. The

quilter's work, which honors, which defers to, and which shows obeisance to its past becomes a visible and material site for holding these memories, as well as a model to inspire future quilters to enact their own very particular brand of remembering.

As such, the character of the quilt is as complex and layered as the work itself. In re-creating traditional design patterns, confined to the medium of fabrics and threads, the quilter literally remembers through the history of her work's involved patterns and colorful designs. And by re-creating those same designs, the quilter bridges the gap between her past and her present, that place where forgetting can take place. If the quilt is a site for remembering, it is also a site which actively blocks the work of forgetting.

The quilter arrests the work of forgetting in three ways. First, she shows herself bound by a duty to remember an aesthetic and craft past. She shows her intention to gather the segments of this past and to piece them together to form a wholly new work. In the act of referring to and imitating quilting's historic trove of designs and stitching patterns, the quilter makes its legacy her own. She makes it her own memory site.

Secondly, the quilter also creates an archive much like a dictionary or manual. Like such books, the quilt is a portable source for remembering through its material parts, its scraps of fabric, which are singly nondescript, even ordinary, but whose patterned sum creates a visual extravagance of achievement. The quilt's own construction becomes its testament. It is an archive of women's creative practices and their rituals for coming together.

And like the books, the quilt can be transported from place to place, from room to room, where the quilting information that it displays is ever apparent. Its stitches and complex designs remain secure and bound within its confines of fabric and threads.

Thirdly and perhaps most significantly, the quilt is a symbolic refuge. It represents a site of a silent pilgrimage for a very private reflection. It provides that refuge within its folds and its surface textures. The quilt becomes a contemplative place where we find comfort. The quilt invites us to wonder. What were the maker's circumstances? Did many of her friends and relatives come to help her sew? What occasions did the fabric pieces mark? What were they — a dress, a tablecloth, a collar? These are the questions we ask each time we look at a quilt. As an object of the everyday, the quilt remains a modest and composed piece. It provides a site for an act of remembering, but one that in this case is not predetermined. Rather, the memories and contemplations the quilt inspires are as varied as each person who makes, looks at, or uses it.

In the end, each quilt reflects a unique inspiration. By its nature the quilt inspires multiple, specific memories. The quilt is a quiet thing of beauty, whose body of layers and fabric scraps force us to remember on both a communal and a very personal level. It helps us to think about the single person who made it as much as it helps us to think about the group of women that may have congregated to sew its pieces together. It reminds us of our social heritage and each maker's individual artistry and creative impulse. And because of this layered richness, the quilt is equally profound and bold, quiet and explosive. It is a complex piece where we return again and again to see, to appreciate, to contemplate, but above all, to remember.

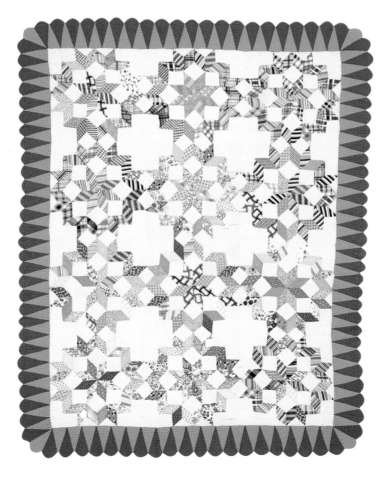

A Word About York County Quilts . . .

The driving motivation of the Documentation was to discover what best represented quilts in York County, not only through the beauty and character of their tops, but also through the composition and components of the individual quilt. A quilt is the sum of its parts, and determining the fabric content, thread, batting, quilting stitches, and innumerable other factors that went into its making speaks volumes about the lives and circumstances of its maker. We discovered quilts that represent every age, every walk of life, every economic level of the community, but the common bond was the love and care that went into the construction of each.

From the nearly 1600 quilts examined, there was no signature style or color palette which dominated. This observation mirrors patterns found in previous studies of York County decorative arts: that the county's geographic position as a commercial crossroads, bringing influences from both Baltimore and Philadelphia, created a blending of styles. Stylistic pockets did exist, however. In the southern end, closer to Maryland, the Baltimore album influence lent itself to more complex appliqué quilts. Quiltmakers living along the east-west corridor leading toward Lancaster County showed more of a Pennsylvania German aesthetic. Where there were farming communities, we found a high concentration of feed sack fabrics and patterns drawn from farm-related publications.

If there was a key lesson in the project, it was discovering the variety and depth through which York County quiltmakers explored their art.

Chapter One

Appliqué

A quilt was oft'-times ready framed,
Before the quilters came,
All neatly dressed in homespun goods,
In ruffled caps and quilted hoods
Of antique name and fame.

Over time appliqué has been practiced in many different forms, and the Documentation Project has brought attention to the fine examples found in York County collections. "Appliqué" is a term that refers to applying a surface decoration to a plain piece of fabric. It is often called "laid-on work" and originates from the French word *appliquer*, meaning "applied." During the nineteenth century in the United States, it was considered the aristocrat of quilt forms, and reached its peak of excellence with album quilts. The term "album" refers to the practice of assembling appliquéd blocks of different designs into a single quilt, a style that was greatly influenced by the autograph books in fashion at the time. The designs of appliqué quilts ranged from the highly original to the pre-stamped fabrics of appliqué kits.

The earliest form of appliqué found in American quilts is called *broderie perse*, which means "Persian embroidery." This style was highly popular in the late eighteenth and early nineteenth centuries, although the original name was "appliqué applied with buttonhole stitch." Mary Gostelow's book, *A World of Embroidery* (p. 22), states that the term *broderie perse* first gained popularity in England in 1851, with the Great Exhibition in London's Crystal Palace. At that time, anything Eastern or Oriental was fashionable in England and America. Through the *broderie perse* process, quilters cut motifs from expensive imported chintz fabric and sewed them to a plain, less costly, background fabric. In this way, quilters could achieve the look of an expensive whole-cloth quilt while using a minimal amount of the high-priced chintz. These fabrics feature flowers, birds, trees, and floral vases and were arranged either in medallion or repeat-block style. The prints themselves were status symbols. Since this technique required painstaking workmanship, expensive fabrics, and the leisure time to complete, *broderie perse* quilts were produced mostly in the affluent eastern and southern states, which included York County, Pennsylvania.

York County quilters looked to the fabric designs of one of the country's most famous print makers, John Hewson, for their inspiration. In 1774, Hewson, at the urging of his friend Benjamin Franklin, left his native England to establish a print works near Philadelphia. Noted textile historian Florence Montgomery states in her book, *Printed Textiles, English and American Cottons and Linens, 1700-1850* (p. 98), that "John Hewson's startlingly sophisticated and handsome bedspread and quilt centers have long been considered without parallel in eighteenth-century American textile printing." The Court of King George III considered the export of Hewson's knowledge so treasonous that a price was put on his head.

According to Roderick Kiracofe in *The American Quilt: A History of Cloth and Comfort, 1750-1950* (p. 56), there are fourteen known Hewson prints surviving today, including one such treasure in The York County Heritage Trust. Ten prints exist in quilt form — including the York example — two are allover-printed bedspreads that are unquilted, and two are handkerchiefs. The York Hewson print is unique in that its center panel with the trademark urn of butterflies, ferns, and flowers has a printed border. The other remaining Hewsons have no borders. As of this printing, there are several pieces under investigation as possible Hewson prints.

The cost and availability of fabric greatly influenced the composition and quantities of quilts made at any particular time. Before the 1820s, fabric was primarily imported from England, France, and India and was, therefore, expensive. York County's access to those fabrics through the ports of Philadelphia and Baltimore enabled quiltmaking traditions to take root in the county earlier than in more remote areas. By the mid-1830s, calicoes were rolling out of American mills at 120 million yards a year, providing quiltmakers with a wide range of affordable fabrics. The variety, availability, and quality of fabrics expanded after the Civil War, enabling quiltmakers to produce an abundance of quilts in the last decades of the nineteenth century. (Affleck, 1987, p. 11)

During the middle half of the nineteenth century, red and green appliqué quilts became extremely popular in the mid-Atlantic states. These quilts exhibit a high degree of workmanship, both in design and technical sewing skills. Largely made from purchased as opposed to scrap fabric, they reflect the relative affluence of some residents. Their designs feature either one motif that was repeated throughout, or a sampler of motifs. Quilts with four large floral appliqué blocks were also popular during this time and were often finished with elaborately appliquéd borders. Their time of popularity parallels that of the more famous Baltimore album quilts and, in fact, they contain many of the same design elements. Baltimore album quilts are considered the epitome of the album style, and are forever linked by name with the prosperous city where the design originated. The appearance of the Baltimore album style in York County quilts, once again, reflects the proximity of Baltimore to York and its influence on the county's culture.

The early twentieth century saw the rise of the appliqué kit. These kits were produced by many companies, including Bucilla and Paragon, and provided quilters with the opportunity to make a complex, multi-colored floral appliqué quilt without the expense or waste of buying each individual fabric. Quilting designs were frequently pre-stamped on the background fabric. Kits featuring many different types of flowers were available, often with the same floral design offered in different colorways.

During the 1930s, appliqué patterns with sentimental depictions of animals, objects, and people became popular. These include standard patterns such as "Sunbonnet Sue," "Overall Bill," butterflies, flowers, and dogs. One dog pattern was inspired by President Franklin D. Roosevelt's beloved Scottish Terrier, Fala. Assortments of butterflies, petals, and other flower shapes could be pur-

chased through advertisements found in popular magazines. These patterns were also given away free as premiums for magazine subscriptions. Many of these quilts combined appliqué with embroidery. During the 1920s and 1930s, appliquéd and embroidered summer spreads made of muslin-colored feed sacks became popular. These contained no filler or backing, but were finished tops with appliquéd trim covering the seams where they were joined together. These appliqué patterns remain favorites of York County quilters to the present day.

Medallion, c. 1790, pieced and appliquéd cotton, quiltmaker unknown, 98" x 96". The medallion in this Hewson print is the only known Hewson with its own printed border. In memory of Mrs. Elizabeth Reinicker and her daughter Elizabeth Reinicker Herr, gift of her niece, Elizabeth Reinicker Herr. *Collection of The York County Heritage Trust, PA.*

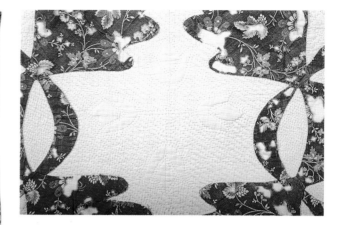

Oak Leaf with Reel, c. 1830, appliquéd
cotton, by Mrs. (____) Crawford, southern
York County, 91" x 91". *Collection of Nancy
and Anne Smith.*

Album, 1851, appliquéd cotton, quiltmaker unknown, 100" x 102". Purchased with funds donated by Evamae and Dale Crist, The Rehmeyer Trust, The Auxiliary of The York County Heritage Trust, and anonymous donors. *Collection of The York County Heritage Trust, PA.*

These beautifully made York County quilts are owned by two museums located nearly 500 miles apart, but they are linked by their similarity of style and by family. Written in ink on the recent acquisition of The York County Heritage Trust quilt are the names John Fulton and James William Edie, both of York County. The quilt in the Shelburne Museum was made by members of the same family and their friends, and presented to John Fulton's sister, Martha Jane. Thirty names are inscribed on this quilt, including the grandmother and two aunts of James William Edie.

The Shelburne quilt is composed of thirty blocks, while The York County Heritage Trust quilt has twenty-five. None of the intricate designs are exactly alike, although a similar touch can be observed. The York County Heritage Trust quilt has a finely appliquéd border; the Shelburne example has none. Both quilts have documented dates, 1851 for the one in The York County Heritage Trust, and 1852 for the one in the Shelburne Museum.

Album, 1852, appliquéd cotton, quiltmaker unknown, 102" x 85". © *Shelburne Museum, Shelburne, Vermont.*

This design was adopted by the York County Quilt Documentation Project as its logo.

Pattern unknown, c. 1860, appliquéd cotton, by Mrs. Mary Yessler Thomas and her daughter Mrs. Bella Thomas Landes, probably Jackson Township, 95" x 95". Gift of Mrs. Bella Thomas Landes. *Collection of The York County Heritage Trust, PA.*

Elizabeth Channell Thomas. *Collection of Richard and Susan Crowl.*

Wall Hanging, c. 1860 (blocks), appliquéd cotton, by Elizabeth Channell Thompson, Fawn Township, 34" x 34". From the original twenty-four blocks, these four (and a twin, not shown) were assembled as a four patch, many generations later. *Collection of Richard and Susan Crowl.*

Left: Moss Rose Variation, c. 1850, appliquéd cotton, quiltmaker unknown, 83" x 82". This summer coverlet features reverse appliqué. *Collection of Sam Meisenhelder.*

Center: Tulip Basket, c. 1850, pieced and appliquéd cotton, by Lizzie Slimmer Baile, Hanover, 92" x 82". Possibly an original design. *Collection of Catherine Baile Shaffer.*

Right: Album, 1854, appliquéd cotton, 83" x 83". Handwritten on the quilt are, "S. Jane Ebaugh, 1854," "A. Hyson," and "John Sutton." *Collection of Edna Hersey.*

Album, c. 1854, appliquéd cotton, probably by Rebecca Garretson Wickersham, Newberry Township, 103" x 101". *Collection of The State Museum of Pennsylvania, Pennsylvania Historical and Museum Commission.*

The Wickersham album quilt is most likely a mourning quilt, made by Rebecca Garretson Wickersham following the death of her husband, John. An inscription on the center block reads, "John Wickersham was born 24 Dec. 1780 died 22 Feb 1853." Records indicate he died of "pulmonary consumption," probably tuberculosis. Next to this center block is one which reads "Rebecca Wickersham was born the 6th day of the 3rd month 1791."

The Wickershams and the Garretsons were among the early Quaker settlers in northern York County. The Wickersham family arrived in the days of William Penn, and was among the founders of the Warrington Meeting, located in the Lewisberry area. Of the fifty-seven signers of this quilt, all are listed in the 1850 northern York County census records, and most belong to the extended Wickersham family.

This quilt is an album style showing a mix of influences from Pennsylvania German folk art and the Baltimore album style so popular in the 1850s. The quilt was carefully composed, with each of the sixty blocks showing a different design. The reel-style blocks laid out in the four corners serve as visual anchors for this work. The flowers have more elements than might be seen in standard Pennsylvania German quilts, yet they are not as complex as the Baltimore album style. Flowers here are flat appliqué, not gathered and folded as in the Baltimore tradition, and the elements are larger than in the Baltimore style. (Cawley, Ezbiansky, Nordberg, 1997, p. 21)

Pattern unknown, 1856, appliquéd cotton, quiltmaker unknown, 74" x 75". *Collection of Deborah F. Cooney.*

Note that the inside Flying Geese border is appliquéd.

Princess Feather, 1857, appliquéd cotton, by
Rebecca Miller (1836-1875), York City, 84" x 84".
Collection of Ruth Smythe.

Top right: Antique Rose Variation, c. 1880, appliquéd cotton, quiltmaker unknown, possibly Emigsville, 80" x 78". *Collection of Kevin and Robyn Strickler.*

Bottom right: Pattern unknown, c. 1880, appliquéd cotton, by Nettie Day Neal, Fawn Grove, 87" x 87". *Collection of Nettie Diehl.*

Top left: Album, c.1860, appliquéd cotton, by the Howett family, Lower Chanceford Township, 82" x 82". Probably made for the wedding of Ann Jane Pyle and William Howett, January 2, 1862. *Collection of David Glenn.*

Bottom left: Pattern unknown, c. 1870, appliquéd cotton, by Mary Wuerthner, York City, 79" x 86". Possibly an original design. *Collection of Doris Givens.*

Laura Laucks. *Collection of Phyllis Koons.*

Rainbow (name provided by family), 1948, appliquéd cotton, by Annie Rauhauser and Elizabeth Hollinger Hull, Washington Township, 79" x 81". Five women in the Hull family put their needles to work to make this replica of a pre-Civil War family quilt. That the original survived is testimony to some clever action. When bands of Confederate soldiers moved through York County before the battle of Gettysburg, pillaging homes and farms, the quilt was hidden under floorboards and in a basement to keep it safe. The original quilt was handed down on one side of the family, but the other side loved the design so much they made their own duplicate, shown here.
Collection of Anna Hull.

Opposite page: Sampler, c. 1920, appliquéd assorted fabrics, by Laura Laucks, New Bridgeville, 79" x 78". *Collection of Phyllis Koons.*

"It is a fearful thing to lead this great, peaceful people into war — into the most terrible and disastrous of all wars, civilizations itself seeming to be in the balance..."
President Woodrow Wilson, Special Address to Congress, April 2, 1917, declaring war on Germany.

Although U.S. involvement in World War I was relatively brief, the war deeply touched York County. Thousands of men and women served; one hundred and eighty-nine died, and hundreds more were injured. Harry B. Laucks, the soldier depicted in the quilt, was counted among the wounded.

Laura Laucks was nearly forty years old when her eighteen-year-old brother, Harry, went off to war. The family had already lost its third-born, Eli, in a 1915 drowning off the oyster boats on the Choptank River in Maryland. No doubt the family feared losing another son.

Although Harry suffered grievous wounds, he came home and Laura commemorated his return with this pictorial quilt. Its "doughboy," Harry, is cut from a piece of his woolen soldier's uniform. The quilt also depicts a Red Cross nurse, perhaps one who helped Harry with his injuries.

After the war, Harry settled in Emigsville and lived there until his death in 1945. Laura lived in New Bridgeville with her mother, Isabelle, and never married. Laura Laucks died in 1940.

Pattern unknown, c. 1920 (quilted 1939-1940), pieced and appliquéd cotton, by Elsie Bott Loucks, Rosa Bott Eisenhart, Sarah Ann Glatfelter Bott, Mahalia Glatfelter Holzapple, and Rosa Glatfelter Gross, 103" x 79". Gift of Walter B. Loucks in respect to the artistry of Elsie Bott Loucks. *Collection of The York County Heritage Trust, PA.*

Opposite page:
Left: Album, 1933, appliquéd cotton, by B. F. Payne and Bertha Hyson Manifold, East Hopewell Township, 84" x 82". Embroidered inscription says, "Papa and Mama, 1933." *Collection of Ann Manifold Zimmerman Wenrich.*

Top right: Dresden Plate, c. 1930, appliquéd cotton, by Louise T. Manifold, Lower Chanceford Township, 86" x 68". *Collection of Deanna S. Johnson.*

Bottom right: Tulips, c. 1940, machine-appliquéd cotton, by Emma Jane Fissel Hoke, Jackson Township, 70" x 70". Both the top and back are made of feed sacks. Each of her seventeen grandchildren received a quilt from their grandmother, Emma Hoke. *Collection of Mary Jo Bollinger.*

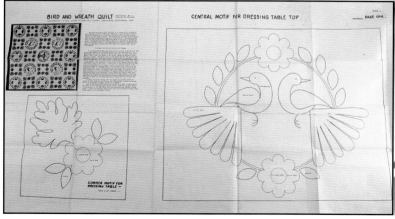

Original pattern called "Bird and Wreath," c. 1940, appliquéd cotton, quilt with coordinating pillowcases and dust ruffle, by Velma Mackay Paul (designer and quiltmaker), Spring Garden Township, 82" x 83". *Collection of Mr. and Mrs. Richard C. Paul.*

Velma Mackay Paul's pattern was published in *Country Gentlemen*, November, 1945. She also published a booklet of her designs. *Collection of Mr. and Mrs. Richard C. Paul*

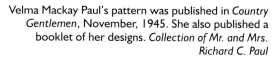

Emily Allen Kain. *Collection of Carol Kain Woodbury.*

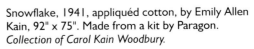

Snowflake, 1941, appliquéd cotton, by Emily Allen Kain, 92" x 75". Made from a kit by Paragon. *Collection of Carol Kain Woodbury.*

Dancing Daffodils, 1942, appliquéd cotton, S. Ellen Sechrist Miller and sisters, York and Lancaster Counties, 96" x 79". Collection of L. Elizabeth Weimer and Virginia E. Brenner.

This stunning Dancing Daffodils quilt is remarkable not only for its beauty, but also because it is very likely the only quilt made by S. Ellen Sechrist Miller. Ellen is said to have started the appliqué work in the late 1930s, and her sisters Lizzie and Maggie, who lived in the New Holland and Lititz areas of Lancaster County, did the quilting. The quilt was completed in time for the marriage of Ellen's daughter, Elizabeth, in 1942.

The pattern is a classic Mountain Mist design that has been offered by the company since the 1930s. The Stearns batting company printed patterns on the back of their Mountain Mist product wrappers to encourage quilters to make more quilts, and, of course, to purchase more batting. In the early twentieth century, commercial patterns began exerting more influence over the look of appliqué quilts. Quilt historian Barbara Brackman notes that beginning in the 1920s, flowers and other images took on a greater realism, and color softened to more pastel tones, like the green and yellow of this quilt. (Brackman, 1989, p. 143.)

For Ellen Miller, sewing was much more enjoyable than quilting. In 1903, the Dallastown resident served an apprenticeship as a seamstress in York, and soon began sewing for the city's elite. Relatives say she spoke of going "in town" for two weeks at a time to make a family's garments, including coats and formal wear. Family lore claims that in the early twentieth century, Ellen made the grandest wedding gowns in York.

With the exception of quilting, Ellen made needlework a life-long pursuit. At the age of eighty-five, she took up crewel embroidery; at ninety-five she learned needlepoint; and she continued to crochet lap robes for her fellow nursing home residents at ninety-eight. Ellen Miller died just short of her one hundredth birthday.

Sunbonnet Sue and Overall Bill, 1939, appliquéd cotton, 105" x 81". Stitched on back: "Made by Mrs. Howard Gray," "Quilted by Mrs. Ada Masters for Gary Otha Gray." Collection of Connie Raab Streibig.

Quilting traditions are most frequently passed from mother to daughter. Often that process requires great patience on the mother's part.

Mrs. Claudine Altland quilted for others, so the quality of her work was important. Twelve-year-old Margaret watched her mother piecing and quilting, and, like most children, was eager to help. Claudine wanted Margaret, her only child, to be involved, but was concerned that her inexperienced stitches were not fine enough. Margaret recalls her mother's simple solution, "She wouldn't let me put a knot on the end of my thread, in case the stitches had to be ripped out."

Margaret's stitches later made the grade, and she was finally allowed to knot her thread. That step tightened the mother-daughter bond and solidified the quilting relationship that lasted the rest of Claudine's life. Later, when Margaret married Monroe Lehigh, he, too, was sometimes incorporated into the quilting effort. He stitched on some quilts, and in fact, a cross-stitched wildlife scene he made was brought in during the Documentation.

Margaret and her mother loved floral patterns, in embroidery and appliqué. The quilt included in this book was a mother-daughter project made from a mail-order kit; Mrs. Altland painstakingly turned in the edges on the tiny flower parts, while her daughter appliquéd them onto the white background with tiny, expert stitches.

Although Margaret no longer quilts for herself, she is still active, quilting as part of the sewing circle of the Pleasant Hill Brethren Church. Once a week, about fifteen church members gather to piece, knot, and quilt bedcovers. Most are given away through Christian Aid Ministries to the children of Romania, but other projects are done as well.

These sewing circles have played a vital role in continuing quilting traditions, and their chief function was to raise money and supplies for church missions. Making and selling quilts was a logical way for these women to fulfill their commitment to help others. Initially, the Pennsylvania Brethren groups would meet at members' homes or spare space in factories, since the church did not allow quilting inside church buildings. That had changed in most Brethren churches by the 1930s, and now some societies have their own purpose-built meeting rooms.

Many sewing circles impose uniform standards on their volunteers, such as stitch size, overall quilt size, quilt patterns, and even specified numbers of pieces for designated patterns. Still, members are encouraged to use their imagination, and to have fun. These works serve as an important outlet for creative expression, and help keep the Brethren community together.

Pansies, c. 1950, appliquéd cotton, by Claudine Altland and Margaret Altland Lehigh, Jackson Township, 91" x 77". *Collection of Monroe and Margaret Lehigh.*

Margaret Altland Lehigh and Claudine Altland, 1990. *Collection of Monroe and Margaret Lehigh.*

Chapter Two

Pieced

The weather and health were first discussed,
And then, at length, the news;
Next was the waning fire rebuilt,
And quilters seated 'round the quilt,
Their forms and figures chose.

York County has an especially rich heritage in pieced quilts. Its early settlement and geographic location gave colonists exposure to both the styles and goods necessary for creating fine quality needlework on a par with other Eastern seaboard communities. Examples of nearly every type of American patchwork were found in the county throughout our Documentation.

The earliest quilts were brought by the immigrants, primarily those of the British Isles. These quilts were simply made by encasing an inner batting between two pieces of fabric held together by stitching or tying. The quilt was made either of a solid color fabric, often a wool, or an allover cotton print, with no patchwork. Although European styles showed elaborate quilting that created a surface sculpture, early American versions generally had more simple cross-hatch quilting, because thread in the colonies was even more expensive than fabric.

In the late eighteenth century, the fashion of the day for bedcoverings consisted of printed whole-cloth designs, such as palampores from India, copper-plated *toiles de Jouy* from France, or polished chintz from Europe or India. These fabrics were cherished to the point that worn chintz draperies might be cut down and recycled into quilts. Owning such bed linens would signify prosperity for the founding families of York County.

For most county residents, quilts were rare items. Raising families and making a secure living consumed great effort and left little leisure time to piece together fabric for quilt tops. Although quiltmakers of the late eighteenth and early nineteenth centuries did piece together fabrics for their quilts, historians like Sally Garoutte (a founder of the American Quilt Study Group) believe that, contrary to common lore, their motive was for artistic expression, not frugality. Likewise, early York County quilts that survive today may have been for show, since they contain a minimal amount of filling. (Garoutte, 1980, p. 19)

Another form of patchwork is the repeat-block style of piecing, where a single motif or design is repeated in rows, a truly American innovation in quiltmaking. The earliest signs appear in the late eighteenth and early nineteenth centuries as borders around a predominant medallion style. The patchwork is either in small blocks, mosaic designs, or in strips as a way to offset the central medallion, which was usually a printed chintz. One York County quilt (shown on page 47) features an astounding thirteen borders surrounding the central medallion.

During the first half of the nineteenth century, American quilters quickly adopted the allover pattern of repeat blocks, which range from simple geometric shapes to very complex designs. In *Clues in the Calico*, (p. 165), Barbara Brackman notes that eighty-six block patterns were used before 1825. By 1850, the number rose to over two hundred patterns. The array expanded even further in the second half of the century, with new variations of established styles.

Even as block piecing grew in popularity, European patchwork continued to influence American quiltmaking. One such example is the English style of paper piecing where fabric is wrapped around tiny paper hexagons, which are then whipstitched together. *Godey's Lady's Book* of 1835 called such a hexagon quilt, "Honeycomb."

The burgeoning popularity of the print media helped spread this new quilt culture. By the 1870s, patterns for pieced blocks were readily available through publications like *Arthur's*, *Peterson's*, *The National Stockman and Farmer*, and *Good Housekeeping*. In addition, commercial firms such as The Ladies' Art Company of St. Louis began selling quilt patterns by mail order. The company stocked hundreds of pattern designs, and in 1898 published a brochure of pieced and appliquéd designs.

During this time, publishers also began giving names to patterns to better market their designs. Many had folksy titles, such as "Hole in the Barn Door" and "Shoofly." Whimsical names were taken from nineteenth-century children's games, such as "Puss in the Corner," and "Whirligig," as well as from popular activities, like square dancing's "Eight Hands Around." Pattern names were also linked with trades and occupations, like "Anvil" and "Monkey Wrench." Some, like "Ocean Waves," "Flying Geese," "Rolling Stones," and "Bear's Paw," reflected outdoor life and nature, and evoked sentiments of the country's westward movement. Some patterns, such as "Drunkard's Path" and "Double T" (for temperance), taught moral lessons. Although women could not yet vote, they did observe the politics of the day, forming opinions and expressing their party loyalties in fabric, in such patterns as "Martha Washington's Star" or "Whig's Defeat." The role of the church, both in religion and community, was also evident in quilting names. "Jacob's Ladder," "Star of Bethlehem," and "Garden of Eden" are a few of the names with Biblical ties. In the twentieth century, some quilt patterns received more updated names. The old Honeycomb pattern of hexagons was given a fresh color scheme and a fresh name, "Grandmother's Flower Garden."

Especially notable in York County are the Pennsylvania German quilts, which were both pieced and appliquéd in many of the popular patterns, but easily recognizable by their distinctive fabric choices. Drawing on folk traditions of their homeland, Pennsylvania German quiltmakers combined colors in a vibrant and unique manner. Color choices ranged from very muted browns to vibrant reds, pinks, cheddars, chrome yellows, blues, and greens. Their primary rule seemed to be "more is better," combining many different colors in a single quilt top. White fabrics, except for the occasional shirting print, are seldom in evidence on Pennsylvania German quilt tops. As a consequence, the vitality of the Pennsylvania German style sets them apart from other quilts made during the same time period. Pennsylvania German quilts are found only in a small section of southeastern and southcentral Pennsylvania, which includes York County.

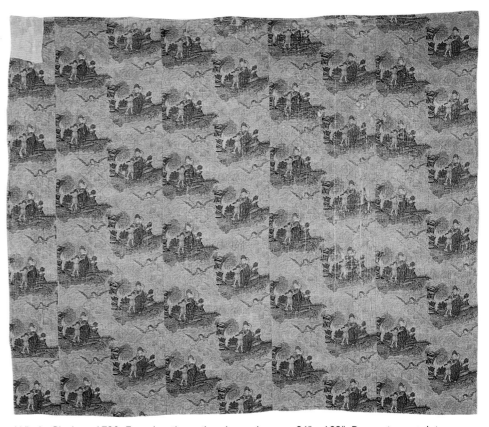

Whole Cloth, c. 1790, French toile, quiltmaker unknown, 86" x 102". Protection patch in upper left-hand corner. Gift of Mrs. Joseph Eastlack. *Collection of The York County Heritage Trust, PA.*

This printed butterfly on the lower left portion of the palampore shows deterioration caused by the dyes.

The flower from the lower left portion of the palampore was appliquéd to the background.

Palampore, c. 1790 with c. 1830 border at bottom, printed cotton panels, quiltmaker unknown, 90" x 70". *Collection of Deborah F. Cooney.*

Tradition holds that palampores, with their elaborate printed depictions of trees, flowers, and birds, were cherished treasures. Owning a palampore was a sign of wealth in late eighteenth century America, particularly for newer immigrants like John Fisher. The palampore shown here was purchased from the Fisher family estate, and was very possibly part of John Fisher's household belongings. At his death in 1808, Fisher was most certainly a man of means.

John Fisher had come a very long way in a very short time. Born Johannes Fischer to a prominent family in Pfeffingen, Germany, in 1736, he arrived in Philadelphia on October 4, 1749, with his parents, a brother and a sister. Fisher's new land was a bitter place at first; his parents died within a few days of each other, possibly the result of a yellow fever epidemic.

Nothing is known about Fisher's early life until about 1756, when he appeared in York. Here he was an engraver and painter, specializing in portrait painting. His only known surviving painting is the Coat of Arms of the Commonwealth of Pennsylvania that was created for the York County Courthouse. Fisher is perhaps best known for his work as a clockmaker. Many of his tall-case clocks still exist, including his masterpiece, an astronomical clock which can run for thirty-five days on one winding. This clock is now owned by Yale University. Fisher is also believed to have made the first pipe organ west of the Susquehanna River. Through his versatility and skill, John Fisher achieved a level of success, certainly wealthy enough to own this prized palampore.

Left: Nine Patch, c. 1810, pieced cotton, quiltmaker unknown, 92" x 80". Bordered in glazed chintz, this nine patch appears to be quilted with homespun thread. Gift of Mrs. Jennie McClellan and Mrs. Elizabeth McClellan Young. *Collection of The York County Heritage Trust, PA.*

Center: Nine Patch, c. 1860, pieced cotton, quiltmaker unknown, 70" x 70". *Collection of Sam Meisenhelder.*

Right: Nine Patch, c. 1912, pieced cotton, by Anna Hull, Washington Township, 76" x 76". *Collection of Anna Hull.*

Anna Hull of the Washington Township area of East Berlin began her quilting life early, though not necessarily by her own choice. She says that by the time she was age six, her aunt, Annie Rauhauser Hollinger, "made her" piece together a nine-patch quilt. It would be a decade before the last stitches were applied, finally finished with the aid of other women in this quilting family. However, Anna didn't stop quilting here. She recalls making about forty quilts over the years, some of them prize-winners at local fairs. Anna never had to work alone if she chose not to, since her sisters Mary Hull Krall and Bertha Hull were also prolific quilters. They often quilted together for friends, family, and community projects.

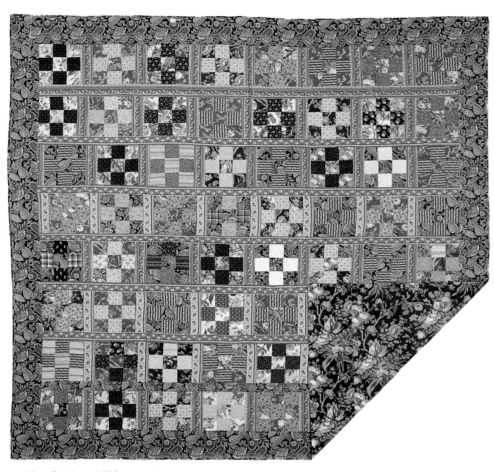

Nine Patch, c. 1900, pieced cotton and silk, presumably made by Mary Alice Hantz Anstadt, 91" x 85". *Collection of Phyllis Hantz Wolf (great-niece of Mary Alice Hantz Anstadt).*

Strippy, c. 1810, pieced cotton with block-printed chintz, 93" x 106". *Collection of The York County Heritage Trust, PA.*

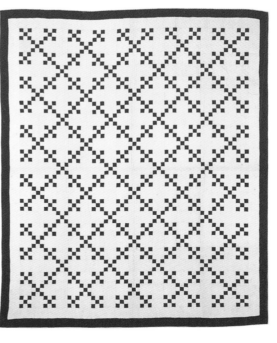

Double Nine Patch with pieced sashing, c. 1900, pieced cotton, by Catharine S. Keesey Edgar, Hopewell Township, 79" x 66". *Collection of Carolyn M. Thomas and Charles A. Thomas.*

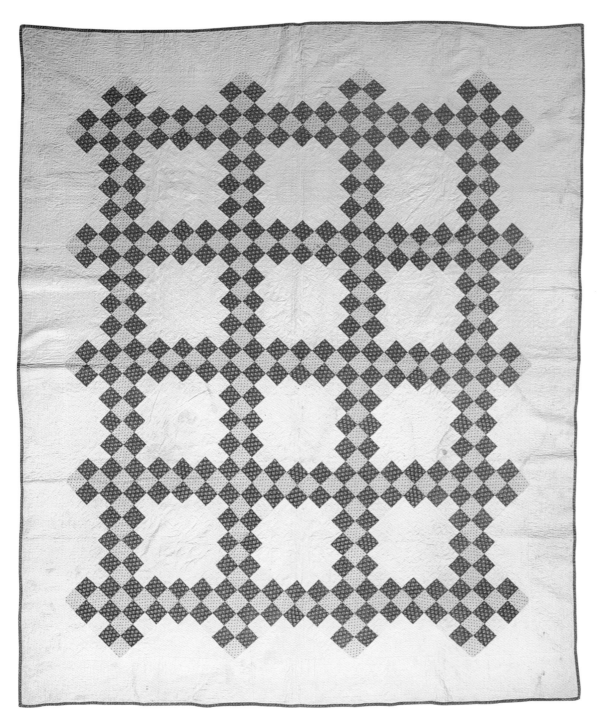

Double Irish Chain, c. 1840, pieced cotton, quiltmaker unknown, 85" x 69". *Collection of L. Elizabeth Weimer and Virginia E. Brenner.*

Lucy Alice Harr Sweitzer with husband Daniel and five of her eight children. *Collection of Marcella Brenneman.*

Double Irish Chain, c. 1890, pieced cotton, Lucy Alice Harr Sweitzer, 75" x 75". *Collection of Marcella Brenneman (granddaughter of maker).*

Triple Irish Chain, c. 1890, pieced cotton, by
Emily Elizabeth Klepper Sweitzer, 83" x 83".
Collection of Jolene Sweitzer Buchart.

Clara Gibbons Wagner. *Collection of Abbie Wagner Wallick.*

Triple Irish Chain, c. 1930, pieced and appliquéd cotton, by Clara Gibbons Wagner, Manheim Township, 79" x 80". *Collection of Abbie Wagner Wallick* (daughter of quiltmaker).

Clara Gibbons Wagner was born in Manheim Township, York County, in 1869, but spent most of her life in the Sinsheim area, around Spring Grove. Clara learned to quilt from her mother, and apparently felt it a tradition worthy of passing on to her thirteen children. Upon leaving home as an adult, each of Clara's ten daughters received two quilts, and each of the three boys received three — just in case they married a woman who did not quilt. Most of these bedcovers were nine-patch patterns, and they often included swatches from outgrown dresses and shirts from her large family. In the last year of her life, she made eleven quilts, one for each living child. Despite Clara's best efforts, however, only one daughter, Alta Arlene, quilted as an adult. Clara Wagner died on April 19, 1942, at the age of 73.

Top left: Medallion, c. 1830, pieced cotton, quiltmaker unknown, 86" x 87". *Collection of Mrs. Karin Jacobs-Caldren.*

Bottom left: Alternating Feathered and Evening Stars, c. 1880, pieced cotton, probably made by Mary Ann Albright Snyder Fisher, Codorus Township, 92" x 91". *Collection of Debra Trostle Bair* (great-great granddaughter of maker).

Top right: Feathered Star, c. 1820, pieced cotton with chintz border, quiltmaker unknown, 106" x 102". Gift of Mrs. Everett J. Gemmill. *Collection of The York County Heritage Trust, PA.*

Bottom right: Ohio Star, c. 1840, pieced cotton with chintz border, quiltmaker unknown, 91" x 89". *Collection of Deborah F. Cooney.*

Annie Kauffman Grosh (1845-1926). *Collection of Miriam Grosh Burkhart.*

Prairie Star, c. 1870, pieced cotton with madder prints, by Annie Kauffman Grosh, Windsor Township, 80" x 78". *Collection of Miriam Grosh Burkhart.*

Medallion, c. 1830, pieced chintz and cotton, by Miriam Woodside Ross, Fawn Township, 99" x 97". *Collection of William Crowl Family.*

Anna Mary with her husband John William Grass. *Collection of William E. And Beverly (Grass) Klinefelter.*

Blazing Star, c. 1880, pieced cotton, by Anna Mary Zinn Grass (1858-1934), 82" x 80". *Collection of William E. and Beverly (Grass) Klinefelter.*

Pattern unknown, c. 1920, pieced cotton, by Mary Grim, Loganville, 82" x 76". *Private Collection.*

Robbing Peter to Pay Paul, c. 1870, pieced cotton, by Daisy Belle Kraber, 91" x 85". *Collection of Fred and Suzon Stauffer.*

Star of Bethlehem, c. 1915, pieced cotton, quiltmaker unknown, 80" x 80". *Collection of Byron H. LeCates.*

Maltese Cross, c. 1890, pieced cotton, by Mrs. Will Lease, 79" x 79". *Collection of Dorothy Roth Warner.*

Margaret Sechrist Hursh with young friend. *Collection of Blanche Grosh Hertzler.*

Joseph's Coat, c. 1930, pieced cotton, by Margaret Amanda Sechrist Hursh, Hellam, 91" x 87". *Collection of Blanche Grosh Hertzler.*

Nettie Day Neal, 1965. *Collection of Royston Neal DeVoe.*

Links of Friendship or Slave Chain, c. 1930, pieced cotton, by Nettie Day Neal, Fawn Grove, 92" x 85". *Collection of Nettie Diehl.*

Star Variation, c. 1890-1910, pieced silk, quiltmaker unknown, 79" x 78". Gift of Mrs. Oscar Heckert. *Collection of The York County Heritage Trust, PA.*

Mohawk Trail, 1949, pieced cotton, by Eliza Jane Bortner Williams,
77" x 75". *Collection of Jeffrey A. Lindemuth.*

Top center: Birth and Baptism Certificate of
Eliza Jane Bortner, 1860. *Collection of
Jeffrey A. Lindemuth.*

Top right: Marriage Certificate of Eliza
Bortner and William Williams, 1886.
Collection of Jeffrey A. Lindemuth.

William and Eliza Williams.
Collection of Jeffrey A. Lindemuth.

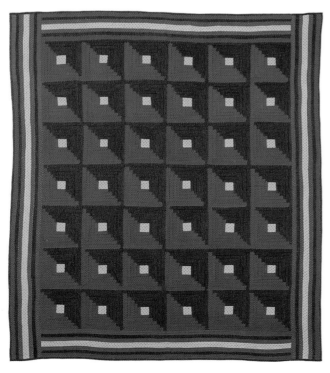

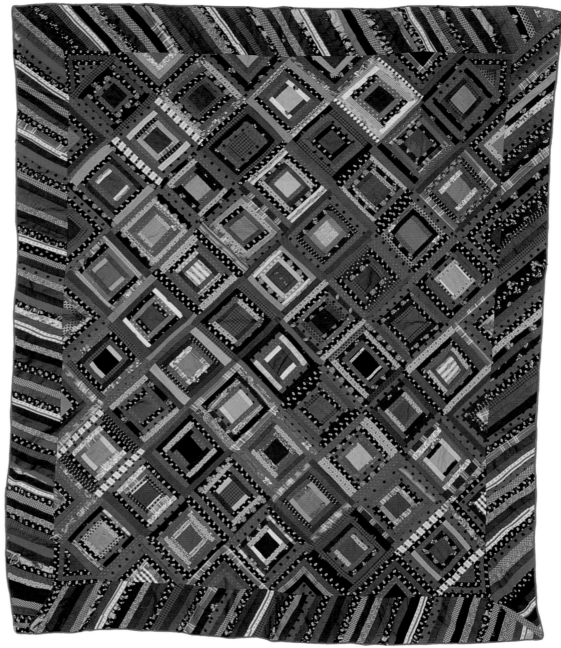

Top left: Log Cabin (Barn Raising), c. 1890, machine-foundation-pieced cotton, by the Lau sisters, 76" x 76". *Collection of Almena Lau* (niece of makers).

Bottom left: Log Cabin, c. 1880, foundation-pieced cotton, quiltmaker unknown, 78" x 68". *Collection of Deborah F. Cooney.*

Above: Log Cabin (Courthouse Steps), c. 1860, foundation-pieced assorted fabrics, quiltmaker unknown, 82" x 68". *Collection of Jacob E. Joseph.*

Anna Miller Forry Stauffer. *Collection of William J. and Joyce H. Strausbaugh.*

Log Cabin (Barn Raising), c. 1890, pieced cotton, by Anna Miller Forry Stauffer, Hanover, 74" x 73". *Collection of William J. and Joseph H. Strausbaugh.*

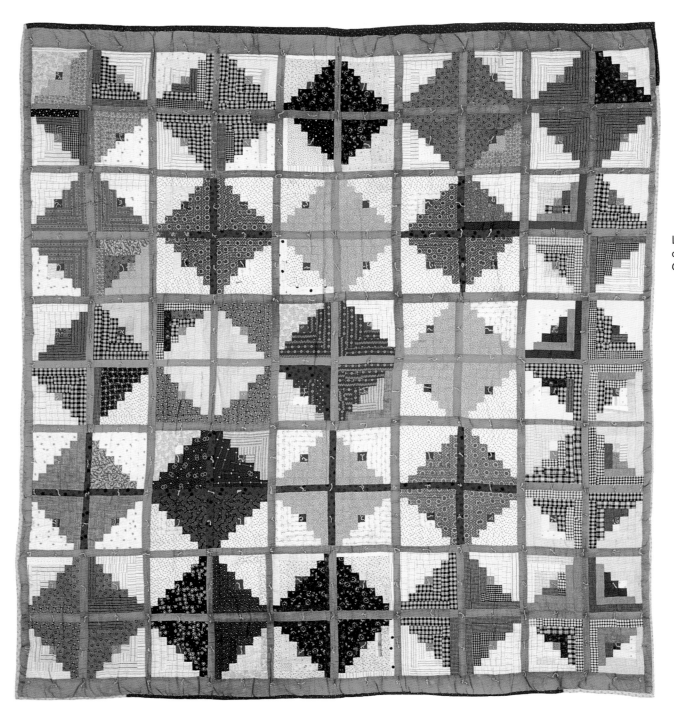

Log Cabin (Light and Dark Variation), c. 1890, pieced cotton, quiltmaker unknown, southern York County, 74" x 69". *Collection of George N. and Joan L. Bair.*

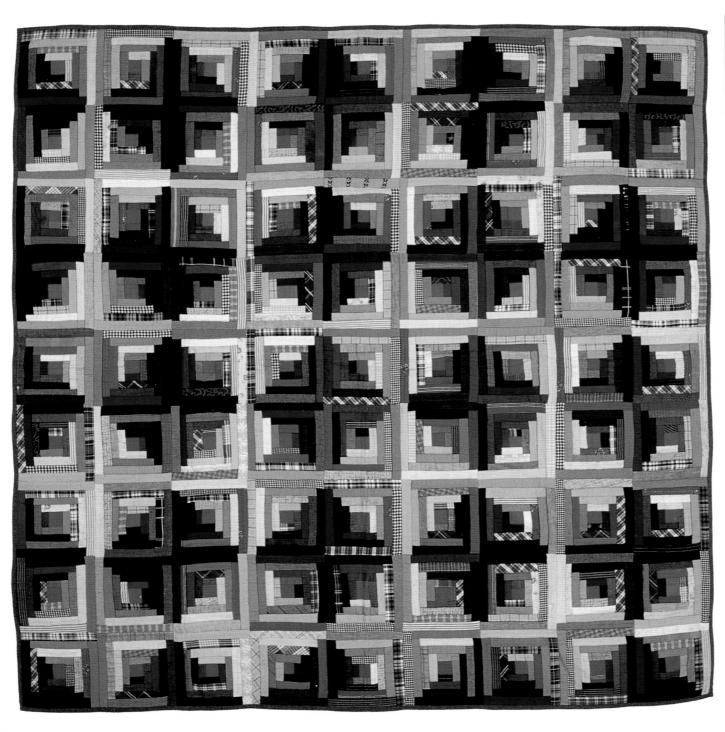

Kathryn Lillich and Alice Louisa Grosscost Fissel at the Pennsylvania Monument, Gettysburg Battlefield. *Collection of Kathryn Grim.*

Log Cabin (Light and Dark Variation), c. 1920, foundation-pieced assorted fabrics, by Alice Louisa Grosscost Fissel, 68" x 68". *Collection of Kathryn Grim.*

Log Cabin, 1940, pieced cotton, Catherine Smith Shearer, 85" x 74". *Collection of Judith Shearer Eisenhart.*

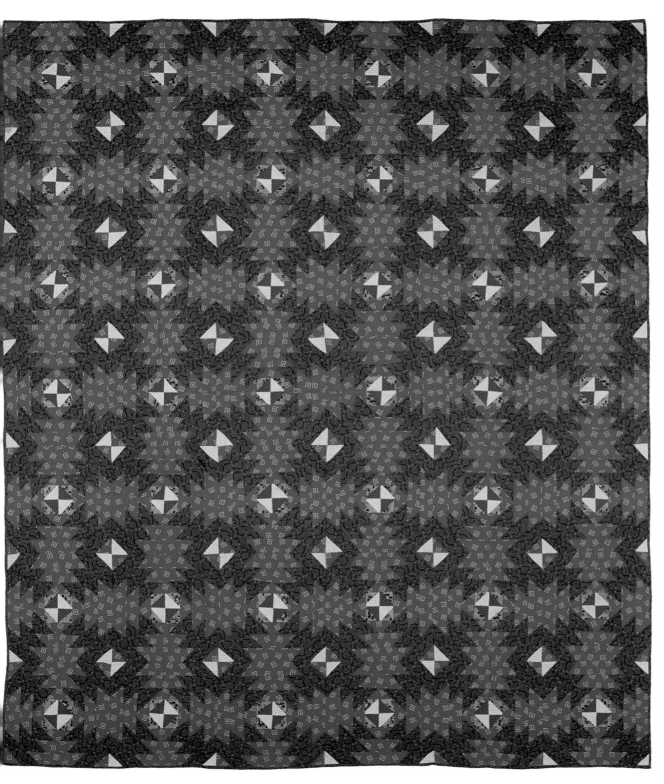

Anna Maria Unger Sterner.
Private Collection.

Pineapple Variation, c. 1900, foundation-pieced cotton, by Anna Maria Unger Sterner, West Manheim Township, 87" x 74". *Private Collection.*

Basket, c. 1860, pieced and appliquéd cotton, quiltmaker unknown, 90" x 101". *Collection of Roberta Benvin.*

Basket, c. 1870, pieced and appliquéd cotton, quiltmaker unknown, 77" x 75". *Collection of Byron H. LeCates.*

Basket, c. 1860, pieced and appliquéd cotton, quiltmaker unknown, 85" x 73". Cottonseeds in batting visible through fabric. *Collection of Roberta Benvin.*

Basket, 1890, pieced cotton, by Laura Martin with her mother Melvina Hake, Manchester Township, 73" x 75". *Collection of Florence L. Sprenkle.*

Basket, c. 1920, pieced and appliquéd cotton, quiltmaker unknown, 87" x 85". *Collection of Byron H. LeCates.*

Double T Variation, c. 1880, pieced cotton, by Alice Trimmer Mummert, Big Mount, 80" x 79". *Collection of Brian Shaull and Lila Fourhman-Shaull.*

Amelia Sauter Weaver. *Collection of Patricia Weaver Strausbaugh.*

Double T, c. 1890, pieced cotton, by Amelia Sauter Weaver, Jackson Township, 84" x 84". *Collection of Patricia Weaver Strausbaugh.*

Eliza Runkle Baumgardner. *Collection of Harry and Machree Baumgardner.*

Capital T, c. 1900, pieced cotton, by Eliza Runkle Baumgardner, West Manheim Township, 86" x 85". *Collection of Harry and Machree Baumgardner.*

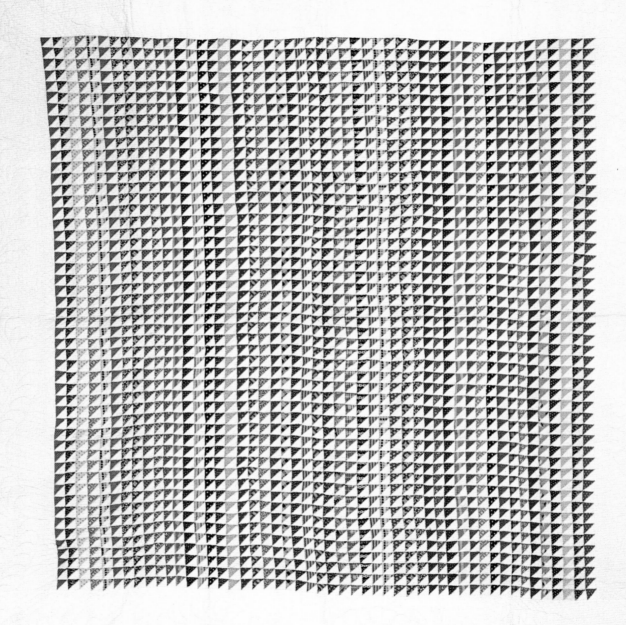

Half-Square Triangles, 1879, pieced cotton, by Mary Jane Ziegler Maish, Windsor Township, 77" x 77". Made when she was sixteen years old, this quilt contains 5,000 small triangles. *Collection of Charlotte Hively* (grand-daughter of maker).

Rebecca C. Heagey, June 1920. *Private Collection*.

Postage Stamp, c. 1870-1890, pieced cotton, by Rebecca Heagey, 86" x 71". Despite the typically random nature of postage stamp quilts, this maker appears to have used a four-by-five block format. The four corner blocks include more cheddar-colored squares than other areas of the quilt, which makes them somewhat distinctive. *Collection of Susan H. Coleman.*

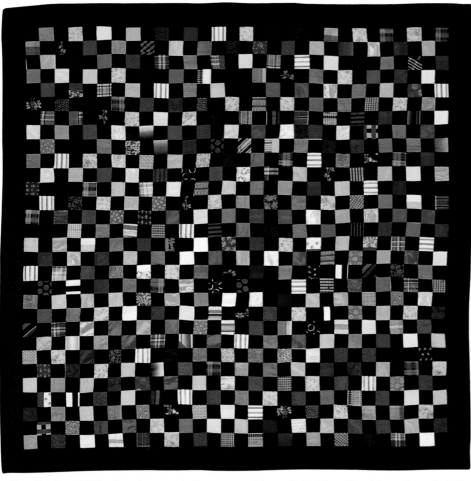

One Patch, c. 1900, pieced assorted silks, presumably made by Mary Alice Hantz Anstadt, 76" x 76". *Collection of Phyllis Hantz Wolf* (great-niece of Mary Alice Hantz Anstadt).

Puff Quilt with ruffle, c. 1920, pieced assorted silks in straight furrow set, presumably made by Mary Alice Hantz Anstadt, 75" x 73" (including ruffle). *Collection of Phyllis Hantz Wolf* (great-niece of Mary Alice Hantz Anstadt).

Hexagon Medallion, c. 1930, pieced cotton, by Mable Immel Doll, Mary Miller, and Mildred Doll Lind, East Manchester Township, 81" x 72". *Private Collection.*

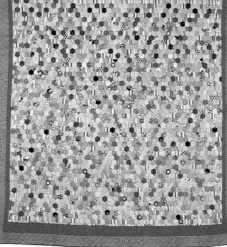

One Patch Hexagon, c. 1920, pieced cotton, by Mary Weaver Troutman, 87" x 76". Collection of fabrics came from a local shirt factory. *Collection of Ann Kroft.*

Trip Around the World, c. 1930, pieced cotton, by Quenton Jesse Markel, Red Lion, 70" x 76".
Collection of Quenton Jesse Markel II.

Any quilt history nearly always becomes a women's history, and, indeed, in York County most quiltmakers were women. However, many a husband, father, or brother participated in the process by building a quilt frame or cutting scrap metal into templates. Some, like Howard McLaughlin or Monroe Lehigh, mentioned elsewhere in this book, helped mark or stitch quilts. In our search, we discovered other outstanding contributions made by gentlemen, and we learned how proud they were to add to this history.

Keeping a farm going in York County during the Great Depression was a challenge, and many families were forced to move to town. So it was with Beulah and Luther Markel. From rural Windsor Township, the family, with three boys, eleven-year-old Elmer William (Bud), nine-year-old Quenton Jesse, and the baby, known as J.R., moved to Winterstown in 1934. There, to occupy the busy hands of Jesse and "Bud" — short for "Budder," the child's version of "brother" — the boys were enlisted to cut squares for quilts.

The following year, the Markel family moved again, this time to a grandfather's home in Red Lion. Bud recalls that on Saturdays, the boys would join their mother in search of feed bags and factory scraps at an ad hoc market that spread out along the main street. There, area residents came to town, selling produce and other wares from makeshift stands, hoping to make a few more needed dollars.

The brothers assembled their quilts with a treadle sewing machine, and Jesse began hand quilting. Sometimes, when the stitches were not up to Mom's standards, the work was done over. Jesse's Trip Around the World quilt has become a family heirloom, but Bud, who became busy with Boy Scouts, regrets never finishing his own.

Both boys appreciated those sewing skills, which came in handy during military service in World War II, when Jesse went into the Navy and Bud served with the Army's 16th Armored Infantry. Bud recalls being recruited often to sew on a fellow soldier's insignia patches.

Another young man, George Koch, learned early the value of precision by marking quilt tops for his mother, Elsie Virginia Rutter Koch. Mrs. Koch was one of four sisters in the Rutter family, which later founded the dairy bearing its name. When their father died prematurely, Elsie's mother helped each daughter cultivate a needlework specialty: embroidery, dressmaking, tatting lace, or quilting. It was her hope that these skills would ensure their livelihood. Elsie Koch frequently quilted for others, as well as her family, and her ten-year-old son George was delighted to help. George remembers laying a yardstick across the quilt top and carefully marking quilting lines in pencil on either side of the yardstick. He was even more excited when his mother let him stitch a bit at the frame in their house on North George Street. "You can't beat that when you're a young boy!" George recalls that his mother, too, insisted that small stitches were a necessity.

Burnell Diehl was just five when he became his mother's quilt helper. The Diehl family had just moved to York from Loganville, and his mother wanted a more fashionable look for their home. Now that the family was in the city — even though East Jackson Street was still unpaved — she decided to make a pair of Grandmother's Flower Garden quilts for the twin beds. Burnell recalls his mother and grandmother sitting at the dining room table at night, cutting the little hexagons for that quilt, sometimes from fabric leftover from clothes. He vividly remembers little piles of those patches, carefully cut out around cardboard templates. Later the twin quilts were given to Burnell and his younger brother, William. Burnell's quilt was brought to the Documentation, but unfortunately, he says, there was "an unhappy ending" to his brother's. In the course of many moves, this quilt became worn and no longer exists.

Quenton Jesse Markel, c. 1935.
Collection of Audrey Markel.

Charlotte Marie Kuhlman and family,
c. 1915. *Collection of Marge Boner.*

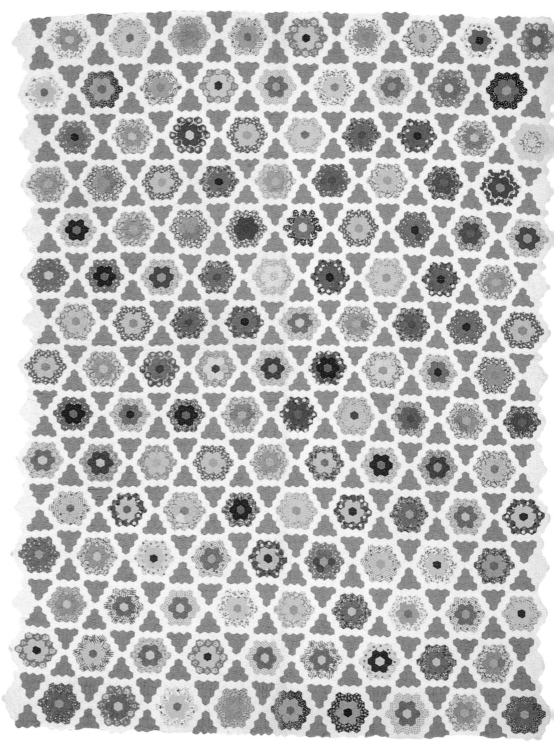

Grandmother's Flower Garden, c. 1930,
pieced cotton, by Charlotte Marie Kuhlman,
York City, 86" x 64". *Collection of Marge Boner.*

Grandmother's Flower Garden, c. 1930, pieced cotton, by Irene Ellen Miller Leese, 75" x 67".
Collection of Cynthia Martin.

Irene Miller Leese was born on October 3, 1901, in Codorus Township, into a farm family that included six brothers and two sisters. Irene loved needlework so much that she often combined "business with pleasure" and took her projects with her as she completed her chores.

In a vivid early memory, Irene recalls losing her crochet hook in a pasture while tending the cows. "I was sitting on a split rail, crocheting, when a calf in the barn started bawling for its mother. That cow took off for the barn, and I took off after her. I chased her up and down and all around, and finally got her back to the pasture. My crochet-work was still on the fence rail, but I never did find that hook."

Irene did not begin quilting until after she married Ralph Leese, on New Year's Day, 1921. While living with her in-laws, Irene's sister-in-law Margie demonstrated the magic that could be created with feed sack and dress scraps, needle, and thread.

Irene's first quilt was a Grandmother's Flower Garden, a popular pattern in the 1920s. This quilt is comprised of hundreds of 3/4" hexagons. To add a special touch, she decided to finish the quilt by turning in the raw edges on the outermost row of hexagons. This ambitious move created a delicate, lacy effect, but the process was so tedious that Irene vowed never to do it again. "I learned to cut 'em off straight, and put on a border." Yet that patchwork pattern stayed with Irene, and her last quilt, completed about 1985, is also a Grandmother's Flower Garden, as were many of the ninety-four other quilts she made.

Quilting was a winter activity, and Irene's frame, acquired second-hand for fifty cents by her husband, was usually set up in the dining room of her home in York during colder months. For quilting patterns, she cut stencils from department store boxes, cereal boxes, and metal scraps. For design inspiration, she turned to the Farm Journal/Farmer's Wife magazine.

On Saturday evenings, Irene often stitched with Margie and, sometimes, a neighbor would join her to cut patches. Once a friend spent the whole afternoon quilting with her, but after the friend departed, Irene judged the stitching so poor she ripped it all out!

Irene once won a dollar for first place at the York Fair, and although she cannot remember the quilt, she does recall that no bank would cash her one-dollar check without proper identification.

Irene Leese made some quilts professionally, but most were sewn for her family, for love. She made quilts for weddings, anniversaries, and new babies, as well as one for each of her grandchildren. And she always seemed to have extras. Granddaughter Cindy Martin says, "When one wore out, you'd go to Grandma's and get another."

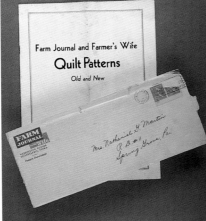

Left: Irene Leese, c. 1936. *Collection of Cynthia Martin.*

Center: *Farm Journal* patterns and mailing envelope, 1942. Irene Leese noted on this pattern, "This is the pattern that I am not making one over." *Collection of Cynthia Martin.*

Right: Irene Leese's metal templates and ruler. *Collection of Cynthia Martin.*

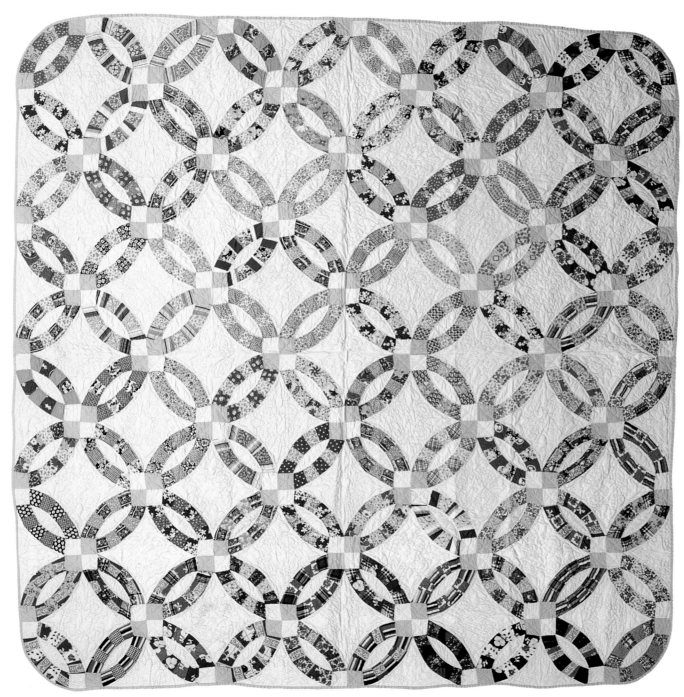

Annie M. Bortner, 1988. *Collection of Donald L. and Brenda J. Gladfelter.*

Double Wedding Ring, c. 1940, pieced cotton, by Annie M. Bortner, Codorus Township, 80" x 77". *Collection of Donald L. and Brenda J. Gladfelter.*

Alternating Rolling Stone with Snowball, c. 1900, pieced cotton, by Lorena Catherine Doll Wildasin, Manheim Township, 80" x 79". *Collection of Carolyn M. Thomas and Charles A. Thomas.*

Nettie Trout Herr. *Collection of Gale Appleby.*

Sawtooth Variation, c. 1860, pieced cotton, by Nettie Trout
Herr, Cross Roads, 94" x 86". *Collection of Gale Appleby*
(great-niece of maker).

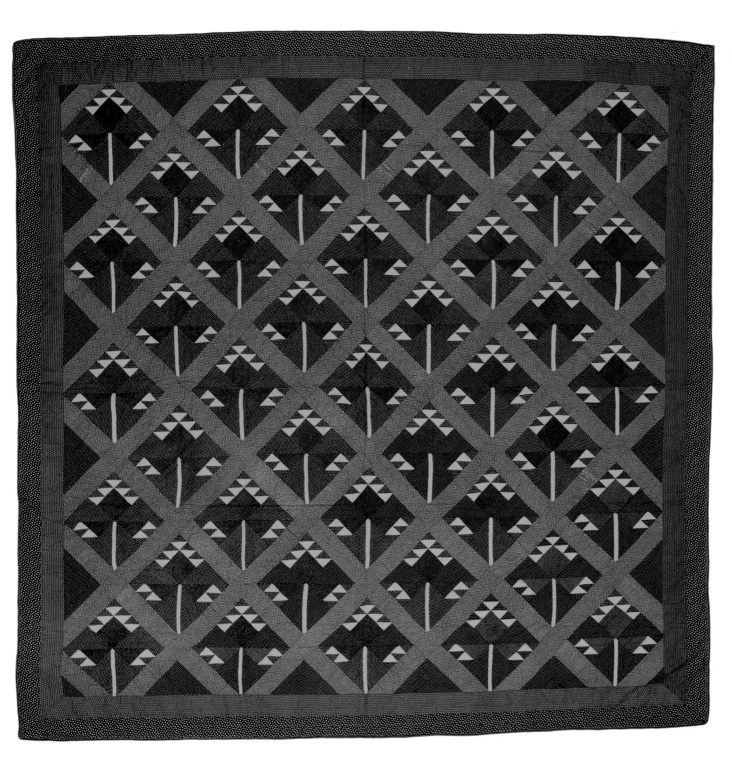

Anna Mary Zinn Grass. *Collection of Evanna Grass Bowers.*

English Ivy Variation, c. 1870, pieced cotton, by Anna Mary Zinn Grass, 92" x 94". *Collection of Evanna Grass Bowers.*

Windmill, c. 1870, pieced cotton, by Mrs. (____) Brinkmann,
Hellam Township, 93" x 85". *Collection of Frances Dietz.*

Blindman's Fancy Variation, c. 1880, pieced cotton,
quiltmaker unknown, 72" x 60". *Private Collection.*

Rebecca Harlacker. *Collection of Mrs. Helena Boring.*

Turkey Tracks, c. 1890 (top), c.1920 (back),
machine-appliquéd and pieced cotton, by Rebecca
Harlacker, Warrington Township, 79" x 76".
Collection of Mrs. Helena Boring.

Road to California, c. 1890,
pieced cotton, by Hoffman family,
possibly Kralltown, 91" x 89".
Collection of Kim Wolgamuth.

Counterpane, c. 1890, pieced cotton, by Alice Trostle Spangler, Paradise Township, 74" x 70". According to the quilt owner, Alice died while doing what she enjoyed the most — quilting. *Collection of Mary Ellen Haverstock Galloway.*

Above: Sewing basket of Alice Trostle Spangler. *Collection of Mary Ellen Haverstock Galloway.*

Right: Alice Trostle Spangler (1855-1932). *Collection of Mary Ellen Haverstock Galloway.*

Below: Quilting pattern cut from the *York Daily Record,* January 18, 1907. *Collection of Mary Ellen Haverstock Galloway.*

Sarah Jane Hoke Markle. *Collection of Mary Jane Day.*

Bear's Paw, c. 1890, pieced cotton, by Sarah Jane Hoke Markle, West Manchester Township, 72" x 72". *Collection of Mary Jane Day.*

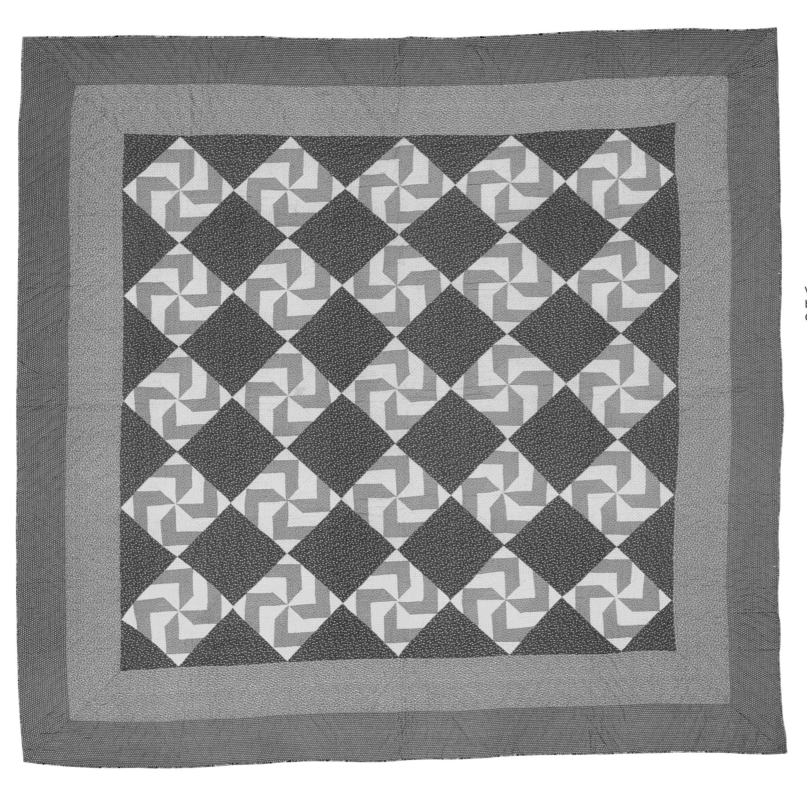

Whirligig, c. 1890, pieced cotton,
by (_____) Spangler, 80" x 78".
Collection of Sandra Bupp.

Lettie Wehrly. *Collection of Vergie Kauffman.*

Twelve Crowns, c. 1890, pieced cotton, by Lettie Wehrly, 76" x 75". *Collection of Vergie Kauffman* (niece of maker).

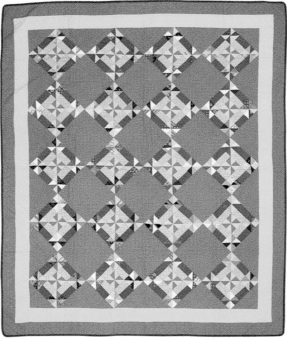

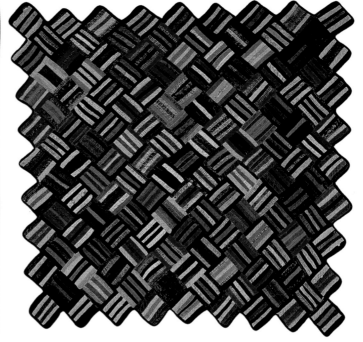

Feathered Squares with Sawtooth Border, c. 1890, pieced cotton, quiltmaker unknown, 71" x 72". *Collection of Mildred Poff Keister.*

Flutter Wheel Variation, c. 1890, pieced cotton, by Caroline Wise (1820-1899), 86" x 72". Made as a gift for her daughter's wedding. *Collection of Carol Stauffer.*

Rail Fence, c. 1890-1910, pieced assorted fabrics, by Margaret Foller (1863-1958), 58" x 58". *Collection of Schell and Peacock Families.*

Louisa Ann Kunkle Diehl (in black dress). *Collection of Janet Louise Yinger Shaffer.*

Milky Way Variation, c. 1890, pieced cotton, by Louisa Ann Kunkle Diehl, East Manchester Township, 70" x 69". *Collection of Janet Louise Yinger Shaffer.*

String-Pieced, c. 1900, foundation-pieced assorted fabrics, presumably made by a member of the Hantz family, 85" x 62". *Collection of Phyllis Hantz Wolf.*

Old Maid's Ramble, c. 1900, pieced cotton, by Martha Yost Raubenstine, Hanover, 80" x 79". *Collection of Martha Raubenstine Stine.*

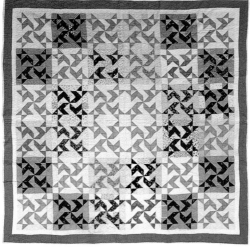

Whirling Pinwheels, c. 1920 (with some earlier fabrics), pieced cotton, by Margaret Amanda Sechrist Hursch, Hellam, 80" x 77". *Collection of Blanche Grosh Hertzler.*

Chained Five Patch, c. 1870, pieced and appliquéd cotton, quiltmaker unknown, southwestern York County, 76" x 76". *Collection of David Helfrich.*

Album, c. 1930, pieced cotton, by Anna Tyson Henry and Emma Dietz, 87" x 85". *Private Collection.*

Lily of the Field Variation, c. 1930, pieced cotton, by Lottie Benedick, 79" x 69". *Collection of Mrs. Martin A. Benedick.*

Eastertide, c. 1930, pieced cotton, by Caroline E. Krone, Newberry Township, 96" x 81". *Collection of Caroline E. Krone.*

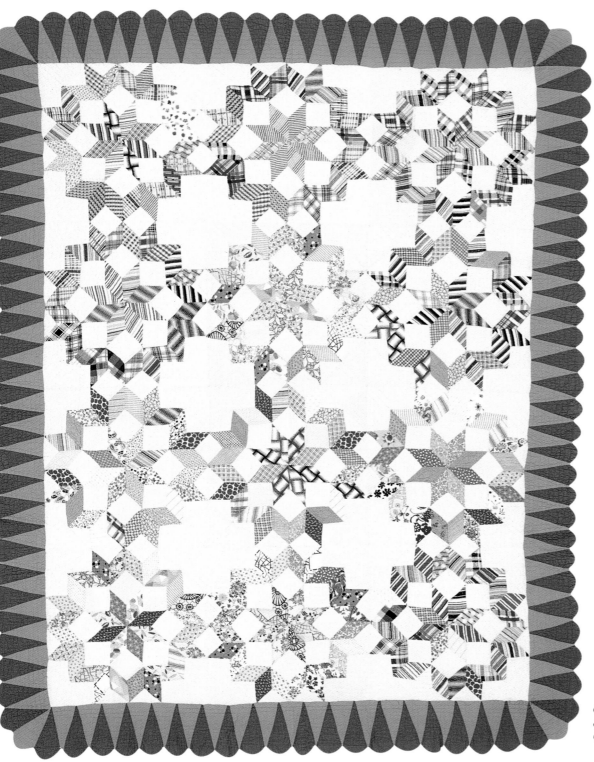

Clara Myers Spangler. *Collection of Janet and John Spangler.*

Octagonal Star or Dutch Rose, c. 1940, pieced cotton, by Clara Myers Spangler, Hanover, 89" x 69". *Collection of Janet and John Spangler.*

Beneath the rich, fertile soil surrounding the towns of Delta and Peach Bottom in southern York County, the early Scots-Irish settlers found another natural resource — veins of slate rock. Beginning around 1840, Welsh miners were brought to the region because of their expertise in handling the huge slabs of slate mined from the quarries. Slate was king in Delta, but while the men were mining the veins of slate, the women were working their own vein — quiltmaking.

Alice Anna McLaughlin Lee represents the mid-point of five generations of quilters in a family that lived and worked on both sides of the Pennsylvania-Maryland border, in the Delta area. The quilting legacy of this family spans nearly two centuries, from Rachel Weeks Boyd, who lived from 1793 to 1848, to Rachel's great-great granddaughter, Nancy L. Smith, an active quilter today. Of her family's craft, Smith says, "It's just something we do, part of our lives." The earliest memories for Nancy, her sister, and two brothers are of playing beneath a quilt in a frame, pretending it was a tent. Quilts from four generations of this family were brought in during the Discovery Days.

Alice Anna McLaughlin Lee was born in Peach Bottom on October 8, 1886, and lived until 1974. She was the only girl of five children born to William Theodore and Anna Mary White McLaughlin. So her mother, her grandmother, and her great-aunt may have felt a special need to pass on the quilting tradition. Alice Lee certainly obliged, creating dozens of quilts in her lifetime.

Alice's father had a colorful business career. In the second half of the 1800s, he pursued several ventures, among them were partnerships in a canning house in northern Maryland, and in a retail butcher shop. Around 1890, William McLaughlin joined with Samuel Whiteford in a store in Delta that sold farm equipment — and explosives. The store supplied the black powder and dynamite used by area slate quarries. Whiteford later quit the partnership, leaving McLaughlin on his own. After his death, William McLaughlin's sons tried running the store, but never achieved their father's level of success.

William McLaughlin dabbled in yet another venture, that of Peach Bottom Township road supervisor, charged with maintaining the highways. In those days, there were no regular road crews, and very few contractors for southern York County. Roads were built or repaired by common citizens as means of paying off their taxes. According to McLaughlin's ledgers, a man could knock a dollar a day off his debt working on the roads, and those with horse or mule teams could earn $1.50 to $2.00 a day.

Alice used not only new fabric in her quilts, but also sewing scraps and pieces from clothing and printed feed bags. Her inspiration for both patchwork and stitching patterns came from the newspapers, magazines, and catalogs she read, as well as the friends and family with whom she often quilted.

Chances are, if you had walked into Alice's house you would find a quilt frame set up in the living room, dining room, or bedroom. You might even be invited to pull up a chair and stitch along. The Tulip Quilt shown here was one such collaborative effort. It was created in the late 1940s, with Alice's brother Howard McLaughlin cutting out the patches, Alice piecing it on her sewing machine, and Alice and her daughter Anna Mary quilting it.

Tulip Basket, c. 1950, pieced cotton, by Alice Anna McLaughlin Lee, southern York County, 89" x 72". *Collection of Nancy and Anne Smith.*

Alice Anna McLaughlin Lee, 1904. *Collection of Nancy and Anne Smith.*

Chapter Three

Signature

And, still, the work goes bravely on —
'Tis work a quilt adorns —
They little dream that 'neath that spread
Some conquor'd hero may lie dead,
Or statesman may be born.

Throughout much of the nineteenth century, signature quilts, also referred to as "presentation" or "friendship" quilts, were a popular way for friends and family to show love and support for one another. Sometimes made to commemorate a single significant event, such as a wedding or retirement, they were also used to acknowledge bonds of friendship, and served as remembrances of friends and family when loved ones moved from a community or joined the westward migration. Many signature quilts were carefully cherished and are, therefore, well preserved. During the second half of the century, signature quilts were also made to promote or raise funds for a particular cause, and are known as "fund-raiser" quilts.

Signature quilts could be either pieced or appliquéd. Sometimes one person constructed all the blocks, at other times, several quilters created their own block to be joined with those of others. As the name "signature" quilt implies, names were applied to the quilt tops, and, in certain instances, dates, towns, drawings, and personal sentiments were included as well. Phrases and poems printed in magazines such as *Godey's Lady's Book,* were also inserted onto the signature quilt's top. One York County example, by a Sarah Ziegler on

her quilt dated 1840, begins, "I only ask forget me not . . ." To increase the sentimental value of the quilt, makers sometimes used a collection of significant fabric scraps, often from clothing remnants, in the quilt's construction. In many instances, the process of collecting the fabrics and assembling and quilting them took years.

The way the names were applied gives clues to the age of the quilt. The oldest quilts included cross-stitch embroidery. Chain stitch and backstitch methods were used later, from the second half of the nineteenth century through the 1940s. Beginning in the 1830s, however, inked inscriptions began to replace embroidery. Although earlier inks were made with iron or tannin, chemicals that caused fabric to deteriorate, Barbara Brackman in *Clues in the Calico* (p. 118) credits Payson's Indelible Ink, which came onto the market around 1834, as the oldest manufactured ink most suitable for fabric. With it, individuals could pen their own names, or a single scribe could write them all, often in an elaborate script.

One prime York County example is the Zion Reformed Church quilt from York City that was made by the friends of the Reverend Aaron Spangler as a Christmas tribute of their love and respect in his tenth year as their pastor. This quilt includes not only the individual names, but also occupations, businesses, and inked pictures, creating a fabric snapshot of life in York in 1883.

Fancy friendship album quilts, the most elaborate of signature quilts, are an extension of the autograph books that families began keeping in their parlors in the 1830s. These quilts, often created with sophisticated appliqué patterns, required much leisure time to make, and thus were seen largely in the more prosperous economic classes. They developed in the early 1840s in the Delaware Valley region of Pennsylvania, but the trend spread rapidly, and it was not long after that quilters in York County caught on to the fashion. Album friendship quilts reached their peak in the 1850s, then slowly faded in favor of simpler designs. (Kolter, 1985, p.10)

Fund-raiser signature quilts became popular in the 1870s, as women turned their attention to causes like the Women's Christian Temperance Union. Communities in York County and around the nation also responded to the Red Cross call for aid during World War I by making signature quilts. Churches were also a favorite cause, and many of these quilts were seen in the Documentation. For a small sum, people paid to have their names included on the quilt. Red embroidered names on a white background was a favorite color combination. The quilts often contain hundreds of names and can be a vital record of a particular church congregation at the time of their making. The finished quilt was sometimes raffled off to raise even more money for the designated cause. In York County, one such quilt was made in 1900 to finance a fence surrounding the cemetery of the Cross Roads United Methodist Church (then Methodist Episcopal). In an unusual touch, each signature also includes the amount of money each person donated to the project. Although these quilts were produced by organizations, such as Ladies Aid Societies, most are now in private hands.

Turkey Tracks, 1904, pieced and appliquéd cotton, by Amanda Elizabeth Gantz Newcomer (1865-1908), Codorus Township, 80" x 81". *Collection of Margaret Rennoll Fuhrman.*

In 1904, fourteen-year-old Mabel Rosa Newcomer of Glen Rock received a special memento of her mother's love — a remembrance quilt bearing the names of two dozen friends. Each friend supplied a print fabric, which Amanda Gantz Newcomer, an accomplished quilter, then fashioned into a Turkey Track block. Mabel's father, William, printed the names of the fabric donors on the white center blocks. Amanda and Mabel also had their own blocks. The initials "MRN" are embroidered in the border. When the top was done, mother and daughter quilted it. On cold nights, Mabel could snuggle under that quilt, warmed by its layers and by the love of her mother and so many friends. The quilt took on an even greater meaning less than four years later, when Amanda Gantz Newcomer died of cancer at the age of forty-two.

Amanda E. Gantz Newcomer, 1885. *Collection of Margaret Rennoll Fuhrman.*

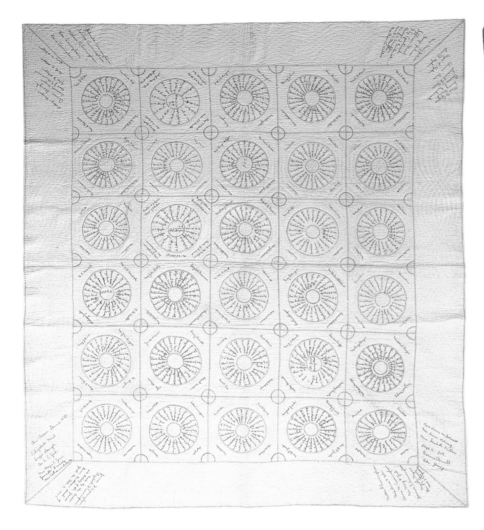

Left: Turkey Red Embroidery, 1905, pieced cotton, by "Ladies Aid Society of St. James Evangelical Lutheran Church of York, PA, Feb. 2, 1905," 81" x 73". Gift of Philip D. Zimmerman and Louise L. Stevenson. *Collection of The York County Heritage Trust, PA.*

Right: Twenty-Five Patch Variation, c. 1888, pieced cotton, by Julian Menchey Leese, Manheim Township, 75" x 77". Julian Leese made this quilt for the marriage of her daughter Alratta Susanna Leese to Noah Theodore Garrett in 1888. *Collection of Anna Mae Bish.*

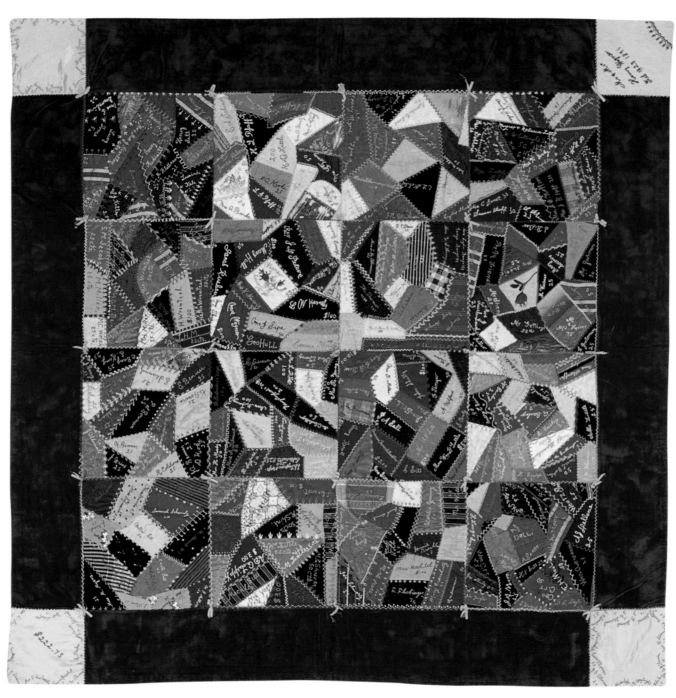

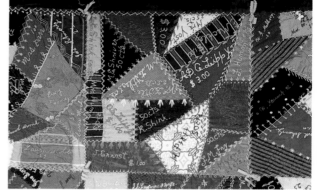

Crazy, February 23, 1891, foundation-pieced assorted fabrics, quiltmaker unknown, Wiota, 67" x 67". Each embroidered signature on this fund-raising quilt includes the amount of the donation. It is tied with gold picot ribbon. *Collection of Susan Hostetter-Cross.*

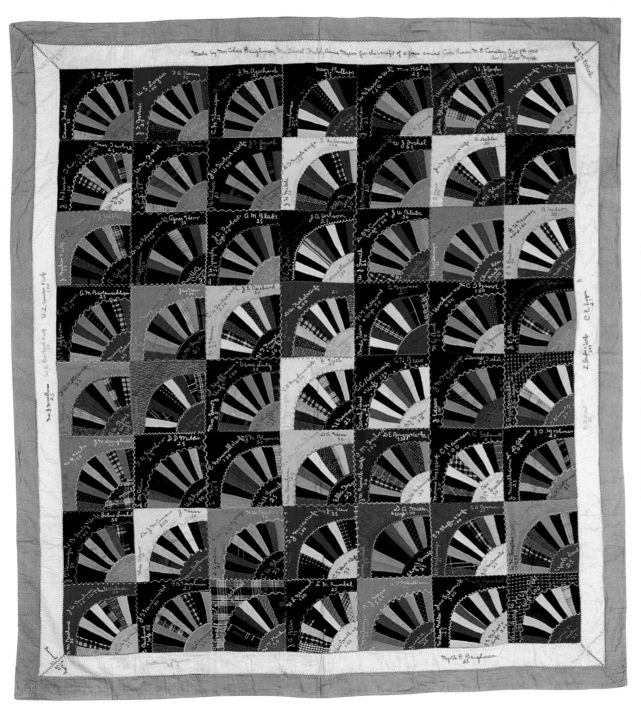

Cross Roads Methodist Episcopal Church (now United Methodist). *Collection of Miriam Logan Seitz.*

Logan's Store provided residents of Cross Roads with their mercantile needs, and possibly the fabrics used for this quilt. *Collection of Miriam Logan Seitz.*

Grandmother's Fan, September 8, 1900, pieced assorted fabrics, by Mrs. Charles Baughman, Mrs. Daniel Fishel, and Miss Annie Myers, Cross Roads, 79" x 71". Funds raised by this quilt paid for the construction of the church's cemetery fence, and the amount of the contribution was embroidered along with the donors' names. *Collection of Cross Roads United Methodist Church.*

Dresden Plate Variation, March 1922, machine-appliquéd cotton, quiltmaker unknown, Brodbecks, Codorus Township, 81" x 81". The owner believes her father, John G. Rohrbaugh, won the quilt, which was made as a fund-raiser for the Sunday School of Jacob's Stone Church, of which he was a member. *Collection of Marie C. Wagner.*

One Patch, 1894, pieced cotton, quiltmaker unknown, Hellam, 86" x 73". Presumed to have been made by four different quiltmakers as a fund-raiser for the St. James Lutheran Church in Hellam. *Collection of Fred and Paulette Toomey.*

Half-Square Triangles, 1883, pieced cotton, quiltmaker unknown, 88" x 89". Presented to Rev. Aaron Spangler at Zion Reformed Church, York, at Christmas, 1883, by his friends. The pen and ink drawings also show the occupations of those named. Gift of Mr. and Mrs. W. Spangler Graby. *Collection of The York County Heritage Trust, PA.*

Embroidered Squares, 1930, pieced cotton, by Ruth Stambaugh, friends and family, 76" x 74". The close proximity of southern York County and northern Maryland is evident in that towns from both states are included in this quilt. *Collection of Ina Ruth Stambaugh.*

Elizabeth Channell Thompson on the right, at her Fawn Township home, c. 1890. *Collection of William Crowl family.*

Album, 1881, appliquéd cotton, by Elizabeth Channell Thompson, Fawn Township, 98" x 95". Except for one signature, Mary Simon, 1881, the rest are labeled 1851. *Collection of William Crowl family.*

Embroidery, 1930, pieced cotton, quiltmaker unknown, 72" x 72". The names of students from the Heidelberg Reformed Sunday School, York, are embroidered with twenty-four names radiating from each block. The quilt is dated February 24, 1930. Gift of Mrs. Herbert C. Hinkel (née Lulu Poorbaugh), one of the class members. *Collection of The York County Heritage Trust, PA.*

Crazy, 1885, pieced and appliquéd assorted fabrics, by The Ladies Aid Society, Trinity Reformed Church, York City, 75" x 75". *Collection of Mr. and Mrs. Gene R. Shue.*

The makers of this crazy quilt, which dates from 1885, not only poured their talents, but also a little of their souls into the project. The quilt was made by the Ladies Aid Society of Trinity Reformed Church in York (now the Trinity United Church of Christ), and presented as an Easter gift to Dr. Jacob Ott Miller, the pastor of that church, and his wife.

Jacob Ott Miller was not a native of York, but became one of its most respected figures in the last half of the nineteenth century. He was born in Woodstock, Virginia, and lived in Reading, Pennsylvania, for part of his childhood. But it was not until 1853 that his Pennsylvania roots became permanent, when he accepted a call to be pastor of the Reformed Church in York.

Just the year before, the church decided to end years of English-German dissension by dividing into two language groups with separate pastors. The thirty-year-old Miller was chosen to lead the English-speaking group, but he soon became a leader for the entire York community, known for his gentle manner and deep understanding.

Dr. Miller's church and civic involvement was extensive. He spent almost fifty years on the Board of Trustees of Franklin & Marshall College in Lancaster; he was president of the Board at the York Academy, which later became York College; and president of the Board of Visitors of the church's seminary in Lancaster. He also served twenty-two years as chaplain to the York City Fire Department, and actively promoted business and industry in the White Rose City.

For his own congregation, he oversaw construction of a new church building and helped bring what had been the German Reformed Church into the American mainstream. York's premier citizens counted themselves as members, as evidenced by the stream of carriages with footmen depositing worshippers for Sunday services.

When Dr. Jacob Ott Miller died on April 18, 1898, at the age of seventy-five, his death plunged the church and all of York into deep mourning. In an unprecedented move, the consistory hired an interior decorator from Baltimore to drape the entire nave and chancel in black. York newspapers gave his passing and his funeral extensive coverage, and commented that it was the largest funeral procession ever held in York.

Rev. Dr. Jacob Ott Miller. *Collection of Mr. and Mrs. Gene R. Shue.*

The presentation booklet that includes all the names of the signers of the quilt. *Collection of Mr. and Mrs. Gene R. Shue.*

In southern York County, a few miles north of Delta on route 851, you will see signs for Bryansville. Today, Bryansville is largely a community of summer cottages for Baltimore residents, but a century and a half ago, it was a town unto itself, with its own post office and a bustling cannery run by the Ruff family.

In 1863, the ladies of Bryansville busied their needles, creating a fine Baltimore album-style appliqué quilt as a gift for returning Civil War soldier, Second Lieutenant Samuel Brannon McLaughlin. The quilt features the cross-stitched signatures and initials of the makers. This gift was not unusual as women throughout the North and South turned their concern and support for their hometown men and boys into the making of a quilt. McLaughlin was born on October 8, 1837, the son of a farming couple, Samuel and Elizabeth Brannon McLaughlin. He and brother John Oliver, better known just as Oliver, worked the family farm until wartime called. In late October, 1862, the brothers joined the 166th regiment of the Pennsylvania Militia, then being organized at Camp Franklin in York. A few weeks before Christmas, the 166th Pennsylvania moved out, heading south to Virginia, at the doorstep of the Confederacy.

The McLaughlin brothers were safely back at the farm before the next growing season was over. Although their war experience was not long, their letters during that seven-month span give a rare Civil War insight into an unexpectedly comfortable life.

In his first letter, on December 15, from Newport News, Virginia, Oliver spoke of seeing the sights in Washington as the 166th passed through. "I saw all the curiosities — and enjoyed myself first rate."

He also wrote excitedly of his determination to go aboard the Monitor, the famed Union iron-clad ship. "I am more anxious to see the Monitor than any other boat I ever herd [sic] of." Samuel also wanted to visit the ship, and in fact, had an invitation from one of its officers, but the regiment received orders to move out to Suffolk before he could go aboard.

From Camp Suffolk, Virginia, the brothers reassured their parents that soldiering was "better than we expected." Samuel wrote, "When I entered camp in York, I weighed 158 pounds, and I can now boast of weighing 171 ½." He said, "We imitate the fat hog — eat and lay down."

Samuel continued, "We get plenty to eat and good. We get bread, beef, beans, rice, coffee, sugar, potatoes, molasses, vinegar, and sometimes dried apples." Butter, fresh fish, and sweet potatoes could also be purchased.

Their pay was as good as their food. Oliver, now a sergeant major, had a base pay of $21 a month. Samuel's second lieutenant rank brought him a base wage of $45 per month. But with expenses for food, clothing, and servant's wages added on, he received $105.50 a month. The McLaughlins employed a former slave, sometimes referred to as a "contraband" in the letters, to help them with daily chores such as cleaning and heating water for washing. They said they were generally healthy, except for Samuel's two-week bout with what he called the "Virginia Quickstep." This ailment seems to have plagued him for the rest of his life — a veteran's document years later notes his complaint of "chronic diarrhea."

In spite of their good reports home, the McLaughlins did witness war. In late January, Confederate forces engaged the Union troops near the Blackwater River. "The cannons are still booming away, and it is twelve o'clock noon," wrote Oliver. The next day, he wrote, ". . . our forces had to retreat, but about daybreak, the 11th Pennsylvania Cavilry [sic] charged on the Rebs, and our men drove them considerably."

At one point the 166th Pennsylvania was put on battle notice against a potential force of seven or eight thousand Confederate soldiers. Oliver wrote his parents, "I want you not to be uneasy for me, as I will feel that God's will must be done, and not mine." He also expressed the belief that his faith would lead him to a better afterlife.

The McLaughlins wrote sparingly of casualties, perhaps wanting to shield their parents. Samuel did write of "25 killed and about 75 or 80 wounded, some 15 of which have since died." Oliver wrote of packed ambulances and drivers so busy they did not have time to eat for a day.

Suffolk was a key location, sitting at a railroad junction leading to Petersburg, and commanding the approach to Portsmouth and Norfolk. In April, 1863, Confederate leaders decided that the Union presence was too great a threat, and General Longstreet and three divisions were sent to lay siege to Suffolk. That siege lasted twenty-three days, until early May, when General Longstreet withdrew and rejoined General Lee on the Rappahannock River. It would not be long before that same Confederate force headed north — to Gettysburg.

During the siege, four companies of the 166th Pennsylvania suffered heavy casualties while trying to roust a nest of Confederate sharpshooters. However, it appears the McLaughlins did not see direct action until May 14. Companies I and D were taking part in a mission to destroy Confederate rail links near Carrsville, Virginia, when rebel forces tried to cut the units off. Both brothers escaped unhurt.

Ironically, about the time in late June that soldiers in gray were riding into Hanover Junction, Pennsylvania — and later into York — the McLaughlins' unit was marching on Hanover Junction, Virginia, with General Peck's force, to cut off northbound rail lines. But despite the intensifying pressures of war, Samuel McLaughlin seems to have retained his sense of humor. He often signed his letters, "No more at present from your son, Samuel B. McLaughlin. Away Down South in Dixie."

Although Samuel and Oliver returned to Bryansville safely, no one is certain where Oliver later settled. According to family lore, he moved out West. In addition to his wartime letters, Oliver is remembered by descendants through several poignant post-war poems that are attributed to him. His "The Old Folks Are Gone" talks about the changes in life, while "Uncle Sam" speaks patriotically of America's broad expanse.

Samuel returned to farming until 1865, when he re-enlisted in the Army, this time as a private. This stint was shorter than his first, lasting only six months.

Samuel married, but little is known of his first wife, who presumably died young. He married for a second time, in 1883, to Mary Jane Norris, a bride half his age. They had eight children, including a son named Abraham Lincoln McLaughlin.

Samuel McLaughlin passed away in August 1908. Mary Jane died in 1956.

Album, c. 1863, appliquéd cotton, by the Ladies of Bryansville, 87" x 86". *Private Collection.*

Second Lieutenant Samuel B. McLaughlin, c. 1863. *Private Collection.*

Detail of letter dated February 22, 1863, from Samuel B. McLaughlin to his parents. *Private Collection.*

Give my respects to all who may inquire for me: Oliver is pretty well to night, he is in the Chaplains tent to night and I think they must have a good deal of fun by the way they are laughing

Give my respects to M Allison and family and tell him that I notice he did not visit us in York this winter

Write soon No more at present from Your Son

Saml B McLaughlin

Away down South in Dixie

Chapter Four

Fads and Novelties

Such conversation as that was
No otherwise was heard —
Where nine good talkers, for the nonce,
All spoke the same thing, all at once,
And each the final word.

Although quiltmaking styles vary somewhat over time, the general concept of a quilt is fairly constant. There have been, however, many fads that catch the attention of quiltmakers for a while, then fade out, only to resurface at a later date.

One of the most recognizable fads, one that dominated quilts in the last quarter of the nineteenth century, was crazy quilts. While technically not quilts — they have no inner batting and are usually not quilted — they are called "quilts" because of their intricate piecing and embellishments. Crazy quilts emerged in the late 1870s as a rejection of traditional patchwork, and they flourished amidst the passion for Japanese artwork and fancy English needle-work like that displayed at the Centennial Exposition in Philadelphia in 1876. The frenzy was also fed by silk weavers, who encouraged the use of scraps for these endeavors. By 1882, *Harper's Bazaar* pronounced, "We have quite discarded in our modern quilts the regular geometric design once so popular." (Kolter, 1985, p.10)

Crazy quilts were designed to showcase a woman's skill in embroidery, ribbon work, and velvet painting. Because they were not utilitarian bedcovers,

many have survived to the present day. The fanciest crazy quilts had either silk, brocade, velvet, or other lush fabrics, highly decorated with elaborate embroidery. Threads and ribbons for these stitches had an extravagance of their own. They, too, were often silk, textured chenille, or perle cotton. Embroidery often included standard motifs, such as fans, butterflies, and for good luck, a spider web. Dates stitched into the quilts help with documenting most of them. A few, however, were commemorative works, created years after an event.

Although fancy fabrics were the standard for crazy quilts, cottons and wools — sometimes from old clothes — were also used. Some quilts included souvenir fabrics or political ribbons. One quilt found during the York Documentation contains a ribbon marking the presidential campaign of James A. Garfield.

The fad of crazy quilts died hard. By 1887, trendsetting magazines like *Godey's Lady's Book* declared, "We regretted much the time and energy spent on the most childish, and unsatisfactory of all work done with the needle, 'crazy' patchwork." However, quiltmakers persisted in using the style well into the twentieth century. (Burner, et al., 1985, pp. 262-264)

Several unique commemorative quilts surfaced during the York search, two made of prize ribbons. One is made from championship poultry ribbons, and the other and perhaps the most striking, is a block quilt made entirely of prizes won at the York Fair in the pigeon competition. Its vibrant palette of bright red, blue, and yellow makes a strong graphic statement on its own, satin prize ribbons notwithstanding.

Another fad, redwork embroidery, began in the 1880s and peaked during the late 1920s and the Great Depression. To make their blocks, women purchased pre-stamped muslin squares or traced their own designs to embroider. Many women adapted simple line drawings found in magazines as patterns to transfer to fabric. Children frequently honed their needle skills with redwork, making covers for their own beds. Early redwork had an eclectic look since it was composed with random combinations of animal, people, and flower designs in a single quilt. These blocks, known as "penny squares," could be purchased, sewn one at a time, and assembled in any order. In the 1920s, themes developed in the designs. Among the most popular series patterns were Ruby Short McKim's Mother Goose and Roly Poly Circus. State flowers, state birds, and flower baskets were also popular subjects. There were many creative uses for embroidery work in quilts, and one that appeared during the Documentation was made of embroidered pictures originally intended to be individually framed for wall hangings.

Yo-yo quilts were also popular during the 1920s and into the late 1940s. According to Virginia Gunn in her article entitled "Yo-yo or Bed of Roses Quilts: Nineteenth Century Origins," published in the 1987 issue of *Uncoverings*, the technique of gathering a circle of fabric dates back to the mid-nineteenth century, but re-emerged seventy years later as a fad. Most yo-yo examples were cotton, unlined, and unquilted.

A fad in quilting even developed from the introduction of a new material. In the late nineteenth and early twentieth centuries, cigar and cigarette manufacturers recognized the market potential of including decorative silk ribbons and flannel patches in their product packages. Women used these to make crazy or patchwork quilts, thus encouraging the purchase of more tobacco. The most frequently seen flannels show national flags from around the world, and one distinctive flag quilt came from the family of a local cigar maker. Cigar flannels were also produced with Native American motifs, such as feathers and teepees.

There have been several popular trends for whole-cloth quilts over the years. White candlewicking — a technique that involves three-dimensional surface decoration made of knots — added a distinctive design element to several whole cloths seen during the York County Documentation. Another whole-cloth fad appeared during the golden days of Hollywood, when many a lady created her own glamour with a "boudoir" quilt. These quilts were created with plush batting and elaborate quilt patterns, and were styled after the home furnishings of the stars of the Silver Screen, a notable example being the peacock pattern that was quilted in cotton sateen. One other whole-cloth variation is "cheater's cloth," fabric printed to look like patchwork. Documenters observed cheater's cloth spanning more than a century. The earliest, a hexagon pattern of 1830, was discovered as the border of an appliquéd quilt of the same

vintage. A unique basket medallion of the 1940s also tested the well-trained eye. Cheater's cloth often reflected the popular patchwork patterns of the day, including stars, Dresden Plate, Grandmother's Flower Garden, Double Wedding Ring, and other motifs.

The unique quilt forms featured in this chapter illustrate the resourcefulness and creative expression that quilters have used over time. While many styles had short life spans, together they represent a vital part of quilt history in the region.

Crazy (top only), c. 1920, foundation-pieced assorted fabrics, by Elsie Rutter Koch, 74" x 76". Elsie was one of the nine original Rutter children born on the site where the dairy farm is today. She grew up not only milking the cows but also quilting and embroidering. She lived in York all her life, married Vincent John Koch in 1916, and had a son, George Albert Koch, who is now the owner of all her quilts. *Collection of George Albert Koch.*

Mary Christina Motter Kraber. *Collection of Richard and Arlene Stauffer.*

Crazy, 1883, assorted fabrics, by Mary Christina Motter Kraber, York City, 77" x 62". *Collection of Richard and Arlene Stauffer.*

Daisy Kraber (on left) and friends. *Collection of Richard and Arlene Stauffer.*

Crazy, 1892, assorted fabrics, by Daisy Belle Kraber, 64" x 49". *Collection of Fred and Suzon Stauffer.*

Quilting was just one of Daisy Kraber's many artistic talents. In addition to fabric, she was equally at ease working with paint, porcelain, and other materials. Family members say whatever Daisy did, she did with a lot of patience and skill. To this day, they display her works with pride.

Daisy Belle Kraber was born on June 21, 1873, to Edwin and Mary (Motter) Kraber of York. She was one of six siblings — three boys and three girls. Despite the family's size, Daisy was never lost in the crowd. She set her own path.

Although she was engaged, Daisy's fiancé died before the wedding could take place. All that remains of this doomed romance is the engagement ring — lost are the fiancé's name, his profession, and his hometown.

For most of her life Daisy lived alone in a house on Country Club Road in York. There, she indulged her artistic pursuits, working to please herself. She painted in oils, and delighted in embellishing plain Limoges china, particularly fruit bowls, with intricate painted patterns. And of course, like her mother, she quilted.

Daisy Kraber's artistic legacy remains a treasured part of her family's heritage.

Crazy, 1890, pieced and appliquéd cotton, by Catherine Smith Shearer, 73" x 65". *Collection of Judith Shearer Eisenhart.*

Crazy, 1890, pieced and appliquéd assorted fabrics, by Annie Loucks Menough, 64" x 64". *Collection of Philip and Kate Pennington.*

Whole Cloth, c. 1900, white-on-white quilted cotton, by Daisy Belle Kraber, 77" x 63". *Collection of Fred and Suzon Stauffer.*

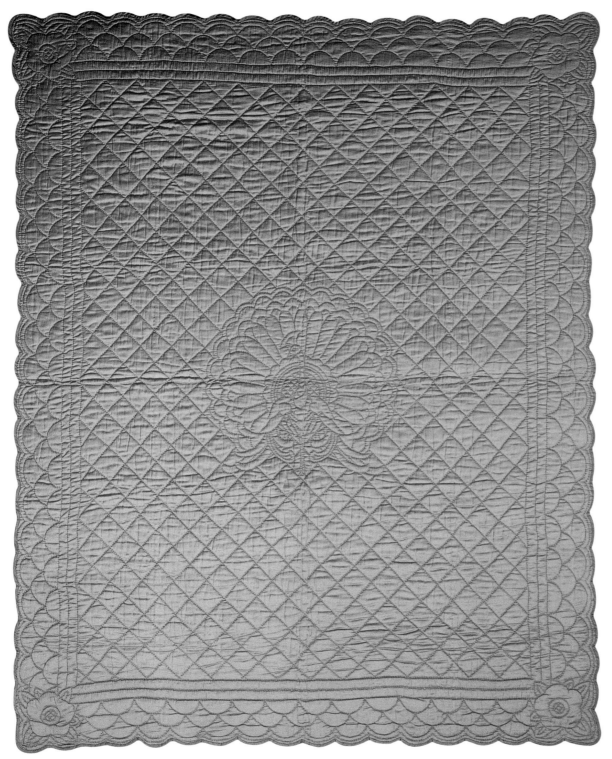

Emma C. (Smith) and William Klinefelter, 1931. *Collection of William E. and Beverley (Grass) Klinefelter.*

Peacock Boudoir, c. 1920, quilted cotton sateen, by Emma C. Smith Klinefelter (1865-1940), 84" x 67" (McCall's Kaumagraph No. 1586, Yellow Transfer Pattern). *Collection of William E. and Beverley (Grass) Klinefelter.*

Original design, c. 1890, candlewicking and embroidery on cotton, The Rev. Jacob Ott Miller and his son Taylor McChesney Miller designed the blocks, and their wives made the quilt, York City, 120" x 92". *Collection of Mr. and Mrs. Gene R. Shue.*

Mary Rishel Meyers, April 24, 1938.
Collection of Bonnie and David Meyers.

Penny Squares, c. 1930, embroidered and pieced cotton, by Mary Rishel Meyers, 80" x 77". *Collection of Bonnie and David Meyers.*

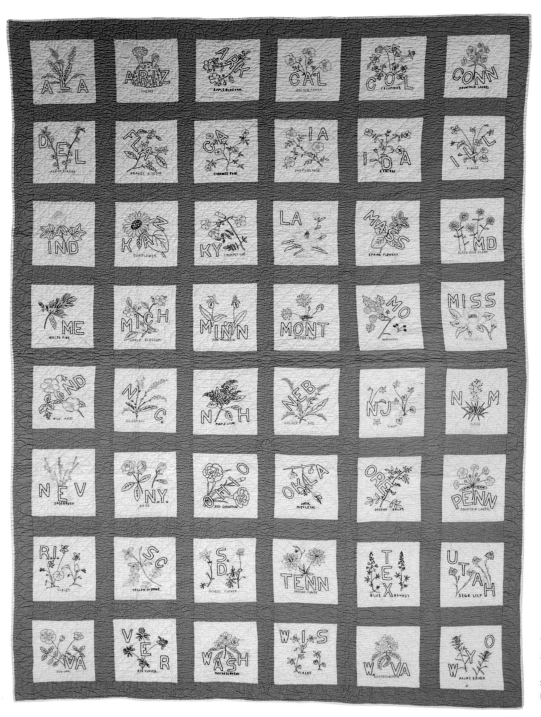

Embroidered Picture Panels, c. 1935, embroidered and pieced cotton, by Mabel Copenheaver Trone, Spring Grove, 85" x 70". The sashing is top-stitched by machine. *Collection of Janet I. Spangler.*

State Flowers (48), c. 1940, embroidered and pieced cotton, by Clara Elizabeth Keeny Thoman Mundis, Springfield Township, 81" x 60". The state flower blocks in this quilt are identical to those in a 1937 advertisement from *Good Stories* magazine, depicted in Barbara Brackman's, *Clues in the Calico* (p. 108). According to Brackman, readers who sold seven subscriptions to *Good Stories* received in exchange forty-eight stamped-muslin blocks to embroider. *Collection of Dennis and Carol Keeney.*

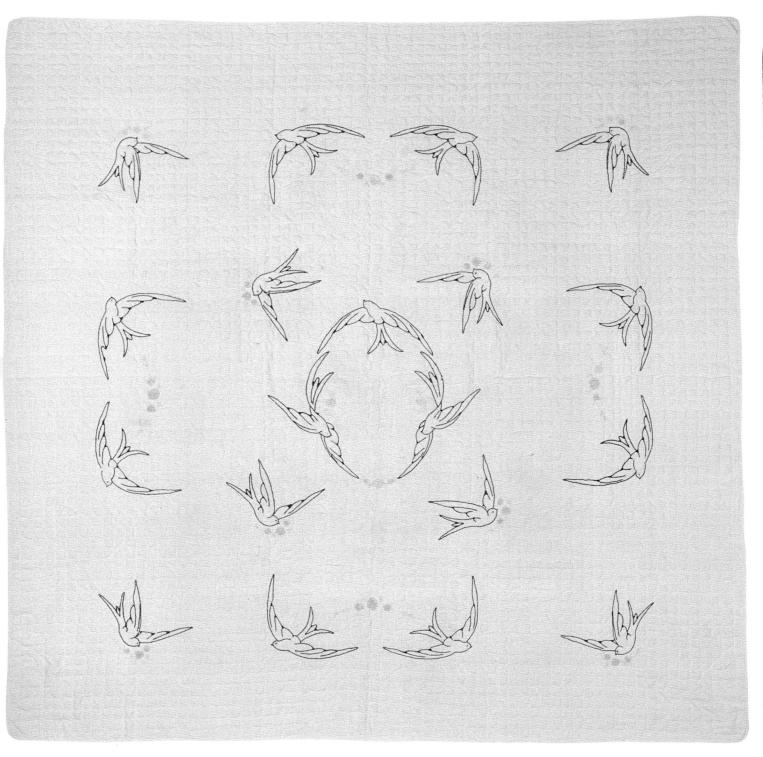

Mahela Berkheimer Dubbs (1871-1958).
Collection of Thomas J. Shellenberger family.

Flying Birds, c. 1930, embroidered
cotton, by Mahela Berkheimer Dubbs,
Hanover area, 73" x 72". *Collection of
Thomas J. Shellenberger family.*

Cross Stitch, c. 1940, stamped embroidered cotton, by Margaret Landis Sipe (embroidery), Lorene Leber (quilting), York City, 93" x 86". *Collection of Diane Landis Bowser and Effie Landis.*

Embroidered, c. 1940, pieced cotton, by Eliza Jane Bortner Williams, 86" x 76". This summer spread includes a wonderful array of motifs, including Dolly Dimple, Sunbonnet Sue, animals, flowers, and other fun designs. *Collection of Jeffrey A. Lindemuth.*

Umbrella Girls, c. 1930, machine-appliquéd cotton, by Amanda Jane Gray Lightner, North York, 76" x 76". *Collection of Sarah Jane Lightner Liek.*

Seen here are cotillion and political ribbons.

Crazy, c. 1910, foundation-pieced assorted fabrics and ribbons, presumably by Mary Alice Hantz Anstadt, 85" x 84". *Collection of Phyllis Hantz Wolf* (great-niece of Mary Alice Hantz Anstadt).

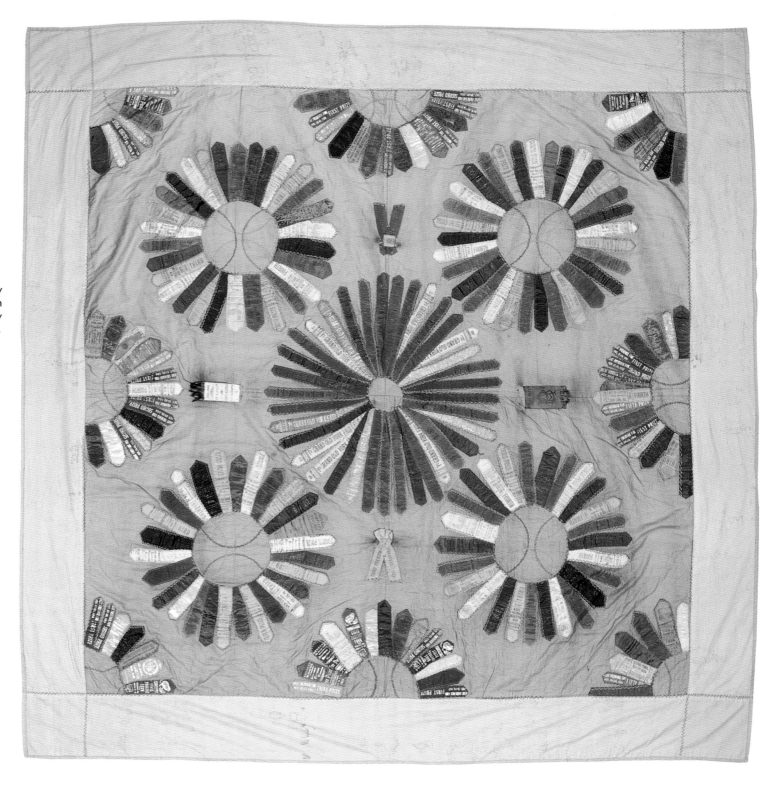

Original design, 1916, appliquéd poultry fair ribbons, 82" x 82". Gift of Ann Buttenwieser. *Collection of The York County Heritage Trust, PA.*

York Fair Ribbons Quilt, c. 1950, foundation-pieced ribbons, by Clara Elsa Elicker, Thomasville, 78" x 75". Made with ribbons won in pigeon competitions by George A. Elicker at the York Fair, 1915 through 1950. Clara Elicker, herself, won a ribbon in 1951 for this quilt. *Collection of Susan Hostetter-Cross.*

George and Clara Elicker, c. 1950, Thomasville. *Collection of Susan Hostetter-Cross.*

1950 York Fair Poultry Exhibitors Catalog. *Collection of Susan Hostetter-Cross.*

Refinement and an attention to detail were hallmarks of the life of Mary Alice Hantz Anstadt. She never missed the birthday of a family member, and she crafted her quilts with meticulous skill. Her Four Seasons crazy quilt demonstrates her dedication to perfection. It is heavily embellished with fine embroidery stitches, plus pictures of birds, butterflies, leaves, and other figures from nature. She apparently loved the crazy quilt pattern, making several more in the following years.

Alice, as she was known, was born in 1867 into one of York's best-known merchant families. Her father, Benjamin Franklin Hantz, was a prosperous and respected hardware dealer whose own ancestors had emigrated from Germany in the eighteenth century.

It is not certain where Alice acquired her talent and enthusiasm for quilts, although this may have come during her education at the Bordentown Academy in Bordentown, New Jersey, ten miles south of Trenton. Her Four Seasons quilt is dated 1885, when she was eighteen, and probably just completing her schooling.

In May of 1893, she married a Lutheran minister, the Reverend William Anstadt, in York. The groom's father, Peter, also a minister, performed the wedding ceremony. The couple lived in York for a time, until church assignments took them to Hollidaysburg in Blair County, and finally to Germantown, now part of Philadelphia. Their only child, a boy, died at the age of three, presumably of diphtheria. In 1915, William Anstadt died in Reading at the age of fifty-two.

After his death, Alice remained in Philadelphia, where the urban environment seemed a perfect fit for this woman, described by family as ladylike, with beautiful handwriting, and a love for all shades of blue, most particularly Wedgwood. She enjoyed taking the Route 23 trolley down Germantown Avenue toward Center City Philadelphia, where one of her favorite destinations was the Tea Room in Wanamaker's department store. Her great-niece, Phyllis Hantz Wolf, remembers joining her there for special occasions.

Alice always sent birthday cards to relatives, adorned with notes in her exquisite script. She also sent gifts, although they were not always hits. Phyllis Hantz Wolf recalls that when she was ten, Great-Aunt Alice sent her a rubber rain cape. With the embarrassment typical of ten-year-olds, young Phyllis balked at wearing the cape, but relented at the insistence of her mother.

Alice Anstadt died in Germantown in 1937.

Crazy, c. 1885, pieced and appliquéd assorted fabrics, by Mary Alice Hantz Anstadt, 72" x 72". The corners of this quilt represent the four seasons, and the quilt is embellished with three-dimensional silk flowers and chenille embroidery. *Collection of Susan Hantz Wolf* (great-great niece of quiltmaker).

Opposite page: Cigar Flannel, c. 1910, pieced cotton, quiltmaker unknown, 58" x 73". This quilt was found in the home of Edith Bergdoll Smith, mother of the present owner, Jesse. Edith's father, John G. Bergdoll, owned Bergdoll Cigar Company, located at 246 East Cottage Place, in York. The company was famous for its York Imperial cigars. *Collection of Jesse and Nancy Smith.*

Chapter Five

Quilt Smalls

They talked of matrimonial things,
And of elopements, more;
And most of all, that latest one?
That cunning one of farmer John
And his belov'd 'Lenore.

In addition to bedcovers, quilters traditionally made an assortment of small fabric items, including crib and doll quilts, pillowcases, pillows, pincushions, petticoats, and sunbonnets.

Historically, quilts have commemorated many of the important passages of life. Crib quilts often celebrated the first stage and were made with thoughts of love, anticipation — and sometimes, unvoiced fears. The dangers of childbearing along with infant mortality rates were staggering during the eighteenth and nineteenth centuries, and it was not unusual for a deceased baby to be buried in a quilt intended to warm him or her through the early years. Crib quilts seen during the Documentation ranged from the very simple and utilitarian to more intricate examples. But an aged utilitarian crib quilt is a rarity due to its hard use. The Mary Emig quilt, made for the daughter of the founder of Emigsville, was a miniaturized version of what lay on adult beds. According to Sandi Fox in *Small Endearments* (p. 39), the Mary Emig quilt may be the only existing example of a Baltimore album in crib size.

The existence of doll quilts reveals America's evolution in its attitude toward childhood. In the second quarter of the nineteenth century, children came to be viewed as beings to be nurtured and educated rather than simply as small adults. As girls received dolls and doll beds during training for their future domestic role, they came to need doll quilts. These were frequently made by mothers, aunts, older sisters, and grandmothers; however, many were also made by the young doll owners themselves as they learned the needlework skills society stressed for young women. Doll quilts might be a leftover block from a larger quilt or a single block made as a sample. Sometimes worn bed quilts were cut down to crib size, then as they continued to fray and show wear, cut down once again to doll size. As with crib quilts, doll quilts generally echoed the patterns, styles, and fabrics of bedcovers for adults. Most are pieced and many from the twentieth century are machine quilted.

Quilted clothing has a very long history, going back to the padded garments that warriors of the Crusades wore beneath their armor. The tradition came to America in the quilted petticoats that were both fashion and necessity for female settlers in the cold New England and mid-Atlantic states. Made of wool or cotton and heavily quilted by hand or machine, petticoats were often passed down from mother to daughter. In early estate listings, the word "quilt" refers to women's petticoats. "Bedquilt" was used later to describe bedcoverings. Two petticoats were brought forth for documentation. One other article of clothing that appeared in the York County findings was a sunbonnet, which was a staple article of clothing on farms. Often its brim was hand or machine quilted for stiffness.

Quilters employed their patchwork talents for numerous home accessories. Pieced and appliquéd pillowcases are distinctive to Pennsylvania during the nineteenth century, particularly among residents of German descent. Pennsylvania Germans have a long history of decorative household items, and the square shape of most of their bedquilts created a need for pillow coverings. To give the bed a unified look, pillowcases were sometimes made to match the quilts, but coordinating pillowcases were made as well. These were seldom quilted. Three pairs of pillowcases were found in the York County Documentation, including an appliquéd duo that is part of a set that includes a quilt and dust ruffle. This set was featured in the November 1945 edition of *Country Gentleman* magazine.

In general, functional pillows or chair cushions were also made of patchwork and quilted, though few had lavish designs. Tabletop covers, on the other hand, were usually fancy, since they were a popular way for women to display their needlework abilities for visitors. Leftover blocks from larger quilts also found their way into the kitchen as potholders or hot pads. These were thickly layered with batting and bound like bed quilts, but were usually unquilted.

Pincushions, a necessary accessory to the quiltmaking process, were sometimes their own works of art, composed of specially pieced blocks that were stuffed. It was not unusual for an ornate pincushion never to be used, kept "just for pretty," a phrase that some older quilters still use.

Arvilla Snydeman. *Collection of D. R. Flinchbaugh.*

Penny Squares, 1917, embroidered, pieced cotton, by Arvilla Snydeman, 55" x 42". *Collection of D. R. Flinchbaugh* (granddaughter of quiltmaker).

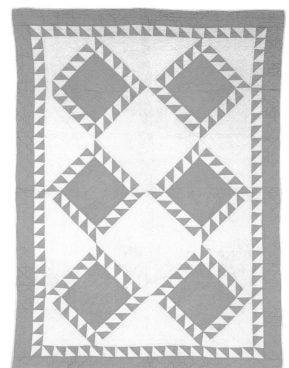

Square with Sawtooth border, 1927, pieced cotton, by Dora Dietz Markley (1870-1969), Springettsbury Township, 42" x 30". *Collection of Jocleta Miller.*

Full-Blown Tulip Variation, c. 1900, pieced and appliquéd cotton, by Rebecca Hantz Snyder, 32" x 32". *Collection of Charles and Judith Snyder.*

Trip Around the World, c. 1880, pieced cotton, from the Livingston family, Dillsburg area, 40" x 40". *Collection of Susan Lutz.*

Eight-Pointed Star, c. 1880, pieced cotton, quiltmaker unknown, 45" x 48". *Collection of Jennie Lehman.*

Annie Nelson Billet, 1939. *Collection of Mr. and Mrs. William Billett.*

Tulip Basket, c. 1930, pieced cotton, by Annie Nelson Billett, Monaghan Township, 38" x 33". *Collection of Mr. and Mrs. William Billett.*

This child's quilt was made by Annie Nelson Billett before the birth of her first child, William N. Billett (born April 2, 1932). She used it for both her children, and then William passed it on to his first child, William N. Billett, Jr. (born October 14, 1953). It was also used for his two brothers and his sister as well as by several of his ten grandchildren.

Embroidered Alphabet, c. 1930, cross-stitched and pieced cotton, quiltmaker unknown, 38" x 39". *Collection of Deborah F. Cooney.*

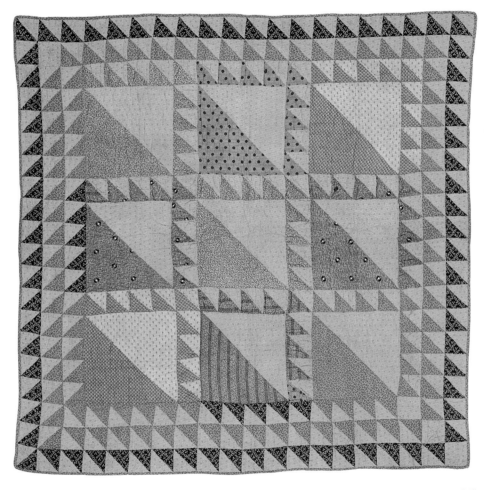

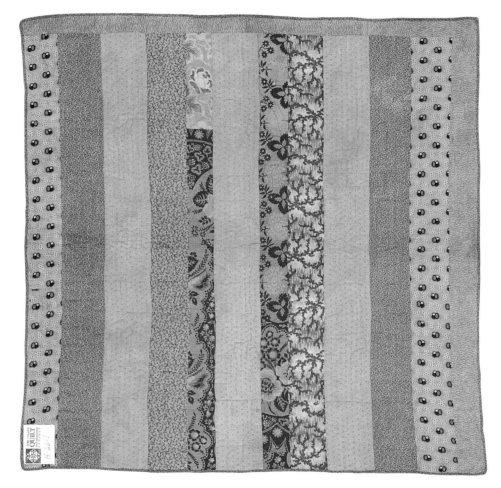

Half-Square Triangles with Sawtooth Border, c. 1860, pieced cotton, quiltmaker unknown, 31"
x 30". *Collection of Deborah F. Cooney.*

Reverse side, in a strippy style.

Log Cabin (Courthouse Steps), c. 1900, pieced wool and silk, by Jenny Goodling, Loganville, 40" x 34". *Collection of Nancy Hershner.*

The daughter of Congressman and Mrs. George Atlee Goodling, young Nancy enjoyed hours of playtime with this c. 1900 doll, cradle, and quilt. *Collection of Nancy Hershner.*

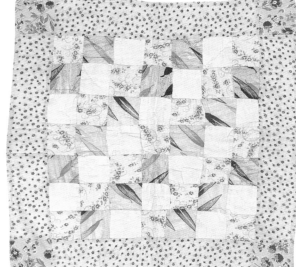

One Patch, c. 1920, pieced cotton, quiltmaker unknown, 19" x 18". *Collection of Suzanne Garrity.*

Rolling Star, c. 1930, pieced and appliquéd cotton, by Clara Elsa Elicker, Thomasville, 19" x 19". *Collection of Susan Hostetter-Cross.*

Sunbonnet with Quilted Brim, 1945, possibly made by Emeline Fishel Snyder. *Collection of Margie Snyder Stover.*

Sampler, 1936, pieced cotton, by "Grandma Throne" (neighbor), North York, 24" x 21". *Collection of Patricia Sipe Seasholtz.*

Pillowcases with Turkey Tracks and Eight-Pointed Center Star, c. 1830-1860, appliquéd and pieced cotton, quiltmaker unknown, 28" x 16". *Collection of Byron H. LeCates.*

Elizabeth Smyser Trostle. *Collection of Mr. and Mrs. Robert Hartsough.*

Quilted Petticoat, c. 1870, silk, probably by Elizabeth Smyser Trostle, waist 27", length 39". *Collection of Mr. and Mrs. Robert Hartsough.*

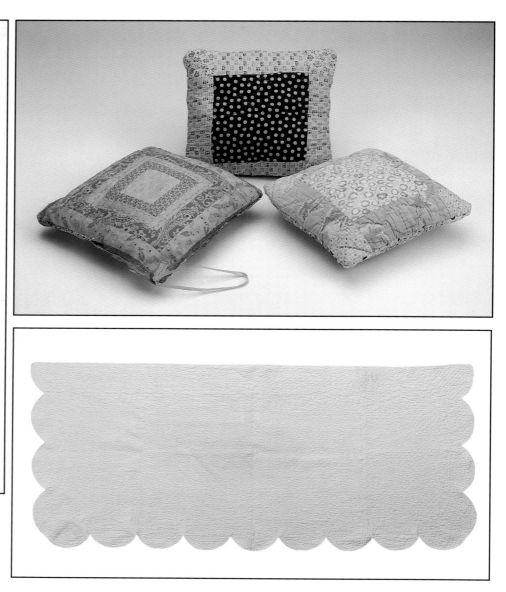

Above: Crazy, c. 1890-1910, pieced and appliquéd assorted fabrics, by Sue Zeigler and her daughter, Maude Zeigler Snyder, 16" x 15". Made as decoration for pillow top. *Collection of Sandra Comer.*

Top right: Patchwork Pillows, c. 1930, pieced cotton, quiltmaker unknown, 9" x 9". The pillow on the left was hung by its loop on a quilting frame and used as a pincushion. *Collection of Wanda Kohler.*

Bottom right: Bolster Cover, c. 1900, white-on-white cotton, by Daisy Belle Kraber, 75" x 31". *Collection of Fred and Suzon Stauffer.*

The tradition of quilting runs strong in many York County families, and one of the finest known York County crib quilts represents one family's heritage. The Mary Emig quilt, which now rests in the collection of the Los Angeles County Museum of Art, was made for Mary in 1847, the year of her birth, presumably by her mother, Sara Ellen Knisley. Sara, who had another daughter, Louisa Ann, was married to John Emig, Jr., the founder of the town of Emigsville. Their home, originally purchased by John Emig, Sr. in 1832, was the Hellan homestead, later known as the Emig Mansion. According to family members, Sara and daughter Mary were involved with the Emigsville Academy, most likely teaching needlework to girls. Sara's other works include an intricate embroidered sampler and a second quilt, a striking Carpenter's Square, that is attributed to her.

Mary Emig remained single, but her sister Louisa Ann married John Brillinger. Although it is not known whether Louisa quilted or not, there is evidence that her daughter, Ellen, born October 14, 1867, did.

On Christmas Eve 1889, Ellen (Ella) Agusta Brillinger and a rising young architect named Harry Bott II were married by Dr. Jacob Ott Miller, the well-known pastor of Trinity Reformed Church in York. Harry and Ella had two daughters. The first, Emma, was born in December 1890. The second, Winnie, was born in 1893, the same year that Harry died, with his daughter Winnie dying a short time later. Sadly, Ella and daughter Emma were now on their own. Ella's life, which had begun as one of privilege, ended as one of hard work.

In the early 1900s, Ella, opened a grocery store at 355 West Market Street in downtown York. Here, she launched a whole new concept of self-service shopping, where customers chose products from stocked shelves instead of asking for them at a counter. With the family living upstairs, the store remained in Ella's hands into the 1920s.

To augment her income, Ella used her needle skills as a professional seamstress, sewing for prestigious York families, including that of Justice Jeremiah Black. She later told stories of being picked up in a horse-drawn carriage and driven up the hill to the Black residence for a day of sewing.

Somehow Ella still did plenty of stitching for herself, often working with her sister Sally, who married Jacob Rutter, a founder of Rutter's Dairy. Ella was said to be jealous of Sally's silver thimble. Ella's cheerful Sunflower quilt was documented during Discovery Days.

Family members say Ella, also known as "Gram," was never idle, always working on one needlework project or another. Dozens of crocheted pieces, from doilies to tablecloths, remain today. In later years Ella lived with daughter Emma and Emma's husband Walter Engdahl. It was there that Emma's daughter-in-law, Nathalie Roth Engdahl, fell under "Gram's" charming spell. Nathalie referred to Gram as a "schlottergantz," a term Pennsylvania Germans use for "free spirit." Nathalie went on to say that sometimes Gram would be "doppy," for example, by wearing two different shoes and neither noticing nor caring. Gram would make fastnachts and lay them on the radiator to rise and say, "Nat, don't we need to test them?"

Nathalie Engdahl fondly remembers Gram's constant stitching. While she lived with the Engdahl family, Gram allowed Nathalie to mark quilting patterns on tops. "But," as Nathalie recounts, "she never let me do any of the actual stitching. Gram wanted it perfect."

Baltimore Album Child's Quilt, 1847, appliquéd cotton, presumably by Sarah Knisley Emig, York County, 59" x 45" (including fringe). Gift in honor of Sara Marie Habib. *Collection of the Los Angeles County Museum of Art.* (M.86.133)

Chapter Six

Construction: The Sum of Its Parts

I hear, methinks, as then I heard,
Just what aunt Betsy said —
"The divil take the blasted witches,
I've lost at least a dozen stitches
By this bewitchéd thread!"

Whether choosing fabrics or patterns, York County quilters kept abreast of the times. Not only did regular traffic on the turnpikes from Philadelphia and Baltimore bring a wide array of materials, even to more remote farm enclaves, but there were also many local resources for inspiration and fabric.

Colonial York was an enterprising community for a variety of trades, including textile production. As early as 1763, a woolen mill powered by an overshoot water wheel operated near the Codorus Creek. County records show that by the beginning of the nineteenth century, many woolen mills were flourishing. For one family, the Heathcotes, their mills were prosperous enough for a town to develop around them, Glen Rock.

York Countians also ventured into the budding American silk industry, perhaps inspired by the 1839 silk convention held in Harrisburg, Pennsylvania. An article from an October 1882 issue of the *Hanover Herald* described the silk business of one John Schwartz, who established his trade in 1848. This article, reproduced in *Labors of Love, America's Textiles and Needlework, 1650-1930* (p. 17), by Judith Reiter Weissman and Wendy Lavitt, stated that Schwartz manufactured 200 yards of silk from his own cocoons, and that he eventually built a

stockpile of 80,000 silkworms. The article continues that Schwartz "passed his shuttle back and forth 9,000 times for every yard of silk he made, which was 27 inches [wide]." In 1900, the York Silk Manufacturing Company's advertising literature noted its specialty, silk that was "easily distinguished by the detachable selvage."

Silk was a favorite fiber for decorative quilts and these quilts often became treasured items within the household. In his handwritten 1873 will, Charles A. Morris wrote, "Item Sixth, I bequeath to my niece, Anna Small, two silk quilts such as she shall select made by her Aunt." Sarah Jane Ziegler Heathcote, the wife of the woolen miller, skillfully used silk in jewel tone colors — possibly from York County mills — to create her spectacular crazy and kaleidoscope appliqué quilts.

Still, as the Documentation project shows, cotton remained the dominant fabric of choice for quilters — in solids, prints, calicoes, plaids, shirtings, chintzes, and cheater's cloth. Other costly and, therefore, less popular fabrics for the average quilter included brocades, velvets, taffetas, and rayon. Less common were drapery fabrics and fur.

Much of the cotton found in the quilts came from feed sacks. It was used both in patchwork and appliqué, for functional as well as decorative quilts. The cloth bags themselves first came into use in the late 1800s for sugar, flour, tobacco, fertilizer, and animal feed. Once the bags were emptied, they were recycled into clothing and other household items. In quilts, feed sacks were used for tops, backs, and sometimes, the filling layer. Bags were often printed with information from the mills, and in many instances, this printing is still evident today. Feed sacks were initially white, however, patterned cotton sacks were introduced in the mid-1920s, in a marketing move. At that time, according to Phyllis George's *Great American Quilts* (p. 189), feed sack makers were being challenged by the rising use of paper bags. By covering their sacks with appealing prints, manufacturers hoped to retain their market, and the trip to the store and the selection of feed became a family affair. Some women recall riding along as young girls to the feed store with their fathers to select the bags they wanted for their new dresses. Feed sacks provided seamstresses with a bounty of fabric, but still, by 1950, fabric sacks were virtually obsolete.

York County quilts demonstrate a variety of construction techniques, some made with great care, others made with speed in mind. The majority were pieced, some by hand, others by machine. When the sewing machine came onto the scene in the mid-nineteenth century, York County quiltmakers quickly grasped onto this time-saving device, launching a new era in quiltmaking.

Walter Hunt invented the first practical American sewing machine in 1834, but never patented it. Elias Howe, Jr. secured a patent in 1846, but seeing little profit, he left for England soon afterwards. It took Isaac Singer to catapult the sewing machine to mass market levels of consumption. He and partner Edward Clark improved the machine, adding features like continuous stitching, a vertical needle, a "light" version for home use, and a foot treadle. These innovations, combined with two flashes of marketing genius, the installment plan and trade-ins, brought the sewing machine into the average American home in ever increasing numbers. (Brandon, 1977, p. 244)

Isaac Singer had strong York County ties. According to the *History of York County* by George R. Prowell, Singer worked as a journeyman tailor under Morton Austin, who had a shop on the southwest corner of Centre Square in downtown York. During the 1850s, three of his children by Mary Ann Sponsler were baptized at St. Patrick's Roman Catholic Church, although the Singers lived in New York at the time. Singer's fourth son, John A. Singer, married Adelaide V. Small, daughter of York lumberman Killian Small. They lived at the corner of East Market and Lehman Streets, in the building now occupied by the Etzweiler Funeral home. By some accounts, at Isaac Singer's death, five women came forward claiming to be his wife. (Brandon, 1977)

Some timesaving quilt techniques of today actually have their origins a century and a half ago. Flip-and-sew foundation piecing was used in the very popular Log Cabin and crazy patchwork designs. Here fabric was used as a base, with pieces progressively sewn on and flipped over until the base was covered. Finished blocks were stitched together, and the seams hidden, either with a strip of fabric or by simply turning the raw edges under. String piecing, another flip and sew method, often used paper for backing, and it was a favorite method for making eight-pointed stars.

York County quiltmakers did exquisite hand appliqué, often developing their own designs and patterns. Some appliqué work is so fine that it gives the impression of being patchwork. Blind hem and blanket stitches were skillfully done, as well. The Wickersham quilt, in the collection of the State Museum of Pennsylvania, demonstrates buttonhole-stitch outlining its appliquéd motifs. In the twentieth century, some appliqué figures were turned under at the edges and sewn down by machine, with the stitching lines hidden by blanket stitching.

Quilt layouts tended to be traditional. There were whole cloth and simple pieced strippys, as well as medallion styles and samplers, with the blocks set square or on point. Crazy quilts had no standard format, but many showed a plan in their design. Log Cabin styles provided opportunities for diverse looks, front and back. Borders ranged from very simple single strips of fabric to complex patchwork and intricate appliqué. A variety of binding techniques turned up during the Documentation, and many were finished by wrapping the backing to the front, and then turning the edge under.

As with piecing and appliqué patterns, quilting designs were handed down through family and friends, or they were acquired through magazines and batting wrappers. York County quilters used what was at hand, making templates out of discarded paper, metal, and cardboard. Empty cereal and department store boxes were often cut into templates.

These thrifty ways extended to fabrics as well, challenging documenters to establish an accurate date for the construction of a quilt. We frequently see blocks, or even snippets of fabric within a quilt, that are decades older than the rest. In addition, well-cared for antique fabrics can be mistaken for reproduction versions, which have a long history of their own. Sometimes, dates were determined through other clues: patterns, batting, thread, and techniques.

The quilts of yesteryear are textbooks for modern-day quiltmakers and historians. Through their study, we can learn volumes about their makers and their origin.

Crazy, c. 1910, foundation-pieced silk, by Sarah Jane Ziegler Heathcote, Glen Rock, 73" x 73" (with ruffle). One small section in this quilt contains pin-tucked fabric that suggests some of the fabrics were reused from a garment. The embroidery thread was perle cotton worked in a feather stitch. Gift of Mrs. Georgia H. Stallman and Mrs. Herbert R. Euler, from the estate of Maude B. Heathcote. *Collection of The York County Heritage Trust, PA.*

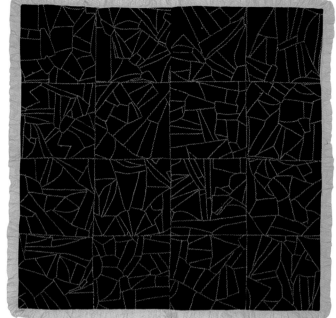

Log Cabin, 1918, pieced assorted fabrics, quiltmaker unknown, 59" x 57". One of the strips of this unusual Log Cabin quilt is a piece of fur. The placement of lights and darks is dramatic. The date "1918" and the initials "SS" are embroidered on the back. *Collection of Suzanne and Dick Hershey.*

Nine Patch with Court-house Steps, c. 1890, foundation-pieced assorted fabrics, quiltmaker unknown, 84" x 84". Alternating the Courthouse Steps block with a Double Nine Patch gives an interesting and unusual layout to this quilt. It is foundation pieced, has no batting, and is assembled square by square. The edges on the back are needle turned. In the corner is "WJPG" in cross stitch. Gift of Mrs. Everett J. Gemmill. *Collection of The York County Heritage Trust, PA.*

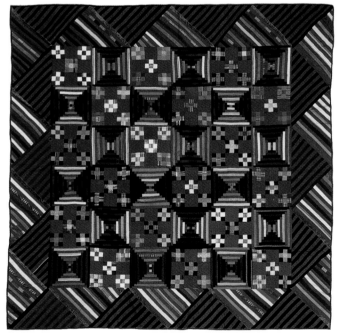

Tulip Variation, 1874, appliquéd cotton, by Susan Wolf Freed, Hellam Township, 89" x 86". Reverse appliqué was used to make the block centers. Each corner is stamped with a name and date, two corners with "Susanna Freed," two corners with "Susan Freed." *Collection of Elaine Doll.*

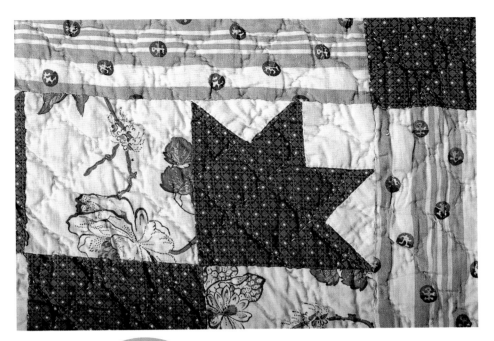

Turkey Tracks, c. 1850, pieced and appliquéd cotton, by Rebecca Forney Lewis, 102" x 101". Close investigation shows that this Turkey Tracks is not patchwork as expected but was partially appliquéd. A small square of fabric was placed in the upper corner of each block and then needle turned into position. Triangles were placed to each side of the square and also appliquéd, thus forming the "toes." Bequest of Elizabeth S. Bonham. *Collection of The York County Heritage Trust, PA.*

York artist Horace Bonham's favorite subjects were ordinary people performing daily activities, and Bonham's world included at least two women who were skilled in needlework. One of these women, Ann Love, a teacher of young Horace, became the subject of a Bonham series, "Threading the Needle." In this study, Mrs. Love was rendered performing the same task, from different angles, in a variety of media. The version here is an etching made around 1881, the same year that an oil painting from the series was shown at the fifty-second annual exhibition at the Pennsylvania Academy of the Fine Arts in Philadelphia.

The second woman, a highly skilled quiltmaker, was his mother-in-law, Rebecca Forney Lewis. Mrs. Lewis and her husband Eli were well known York County residents, Mrs. Lewis having come from a prominent Hanover family, and Mr. Lewis from the town of Lewisberry, which was named for his family. Their daughter, Rebekah, married Horace Bonham in 1870. Rebekah and Horace's home at 152 East Market Street is now part of The York County Heritage Trust, and several of the fine quilts made by Mrs. Lewis are displayed in this museum.

Rebecca Forney Lewis.

Etching of Ann Love by Horace Bonham. *Collection of The York County Heritage Trust, PA.*

Spiderweb, c. 1930, pieced cotton, by Margaret Amanda Sechrist Hursch, Hellam, 83" x 82". In string piecing, one side of a strip of fabric was sewn face down onto paper or fabric and then flipped right side up. Another strip was placed face down on top of it, sewn and flipped. The process was repeated until a new piece of fabric was made that was big enough for the template. Shapes were cut out, such as diamonds in this case, and then sewn together. Eight diamonds sewn together made a star. The star was then either appliquéd onto a background or pieced into one. *Collection of Blanche Grosh Hertzler.*

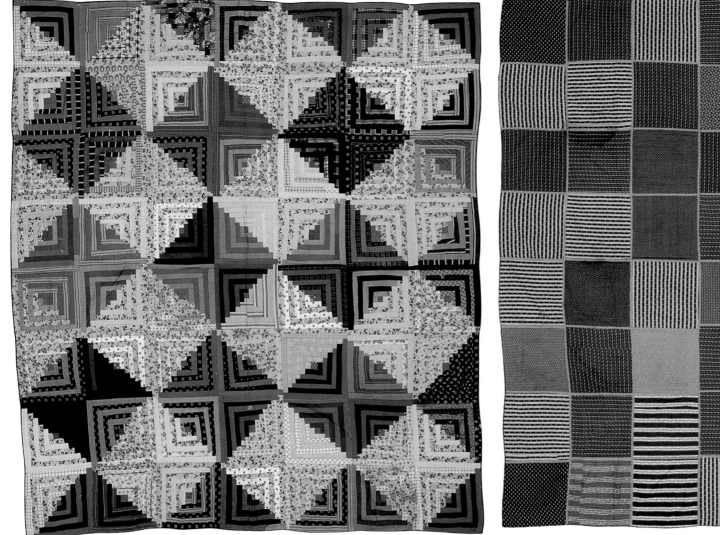

Log Cabin, c. 1890, foundation-pieced cotton, by Margaret Miller Hyson, East Hopewell Township, 91" x 81". In this Log Cabin the blocks are set straight, but the placement of lights and darks make the design appear as though the squares were set on point. *Collection of Ann Manifold Zimmerman Wenrich.*

Reverse side of Log Cabin. This quilt was sewn to a fabric foundation and the seams were covered with a contrasting strip of fabric.

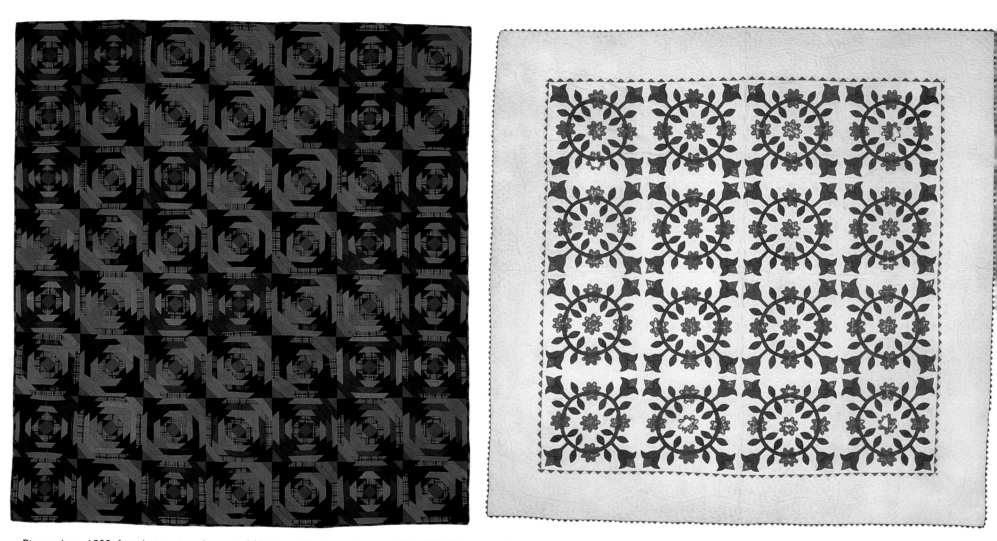

Pineapple, c. 1900, foundation-pieced assorted fabrics, quiltmaker unknown, 87" x 77". This dramatic Pineapple quilt was hand stitched onto fabric foundation squares and then assembled square to square. The seams on the back are covered with an additional strip of fabric. *Collection of The York County Heritage Trust, PA.*

Rose and Tulip Wreath, c. 1850, appliquéd cotton, possibly by Nettie Garrett, Hanover, 83" x 83". A sawtooth inner border and prairie point edge treatment complement the elegance of this lovely rose and leaf appliqué. *Collection of Larry Smith.*

Manufacturer's stamp is still visible on background fabric of quilt top.

Princess Feather Medallion, c. 1840, appliquéd cotton, possibly by Sallie Scott, southern York County, 83" x 84". The simple and graceful lines of this border are a lovely complement to the feather in the center and the surrounding roses. *Collection of George N. and Joan L. Bair.*

Tea Roses and Bells, c. 1850, appliquéd cotton, quiltmaker unknown, 96" x 93". This early album-style quilt features an elegant appliquéd border and sawtooth appliquéd edge. *Collection of Deborah F. Cooney.*

Alice Harlacker Wallace (1862-1935). *Collection of Patsy Elaine Drawbaugh Hartnett.*

Pattern unknown, c. 1910, pieced and appliquéd cotton, by Alice Harlacker Wallace, Dover Township, 80" x 79". *Collection of Patsy Elaine Drawbaugh Hartnett.*

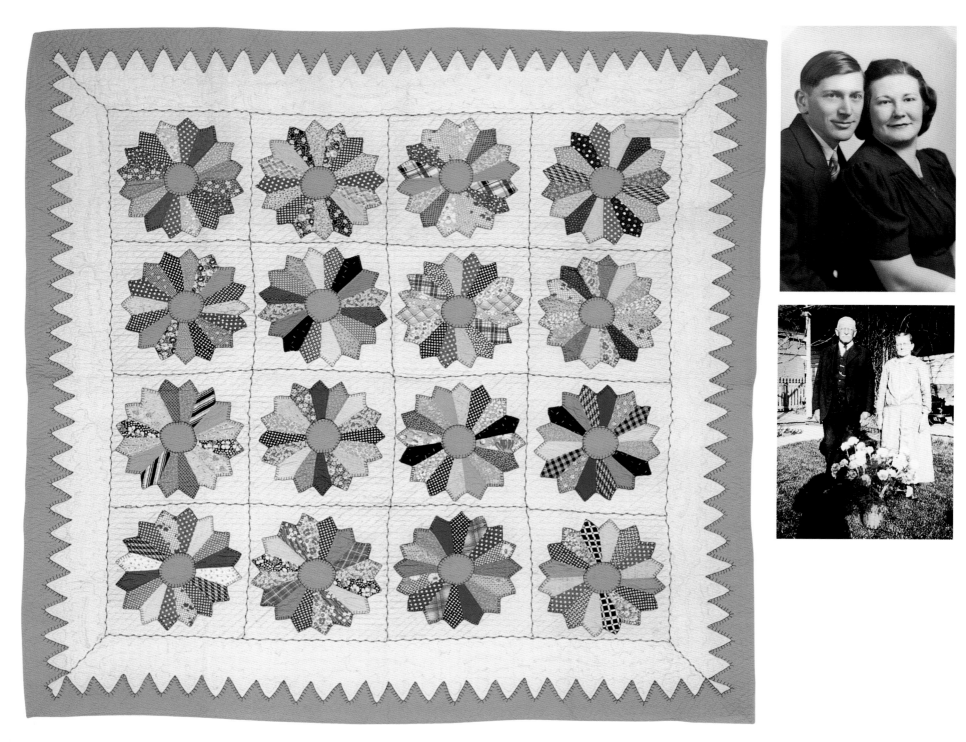

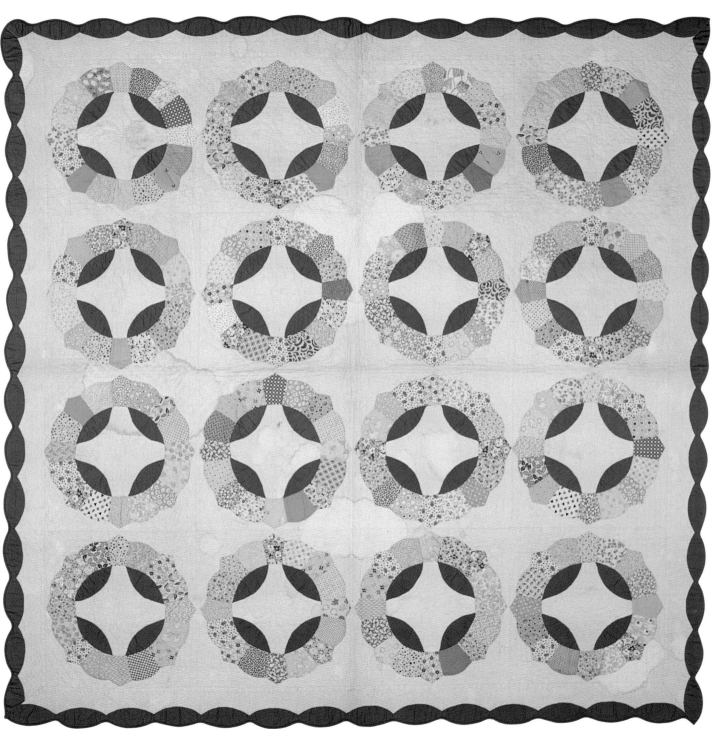

Opposite page:
Left: Dresden Plate, 1936, machine-appliquéd cotton, appliquéd by Luella Shaffer and quilted by her grandmother Sophia Jane Shue Shaffer, 79" x 77". The appliqué border and the way the seams are set off with embroidery make a strong design statement. The appliqué edges are turned under, top stitched by machine, and then blanket stitched on top. *Collection of Paul E. Shaffer.*

Top right: Kurvin and Luella (Shaffer) Lecrone. *Collection of Paul E. Shaffer.*

Center right: "Grandpa" and Sophia Shaffer.

Sunflower, c. 1930, pieced cotton, by Margaret May Herbert Webb, Fawn Grove, 78" x 76". An unusual double-scalloped edge treatment frames this scrappy Sunflower pattern. *Collection of Vincent Curtis and Rheba Evelyn Ingram Webb.*

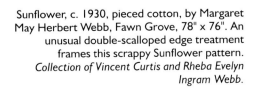

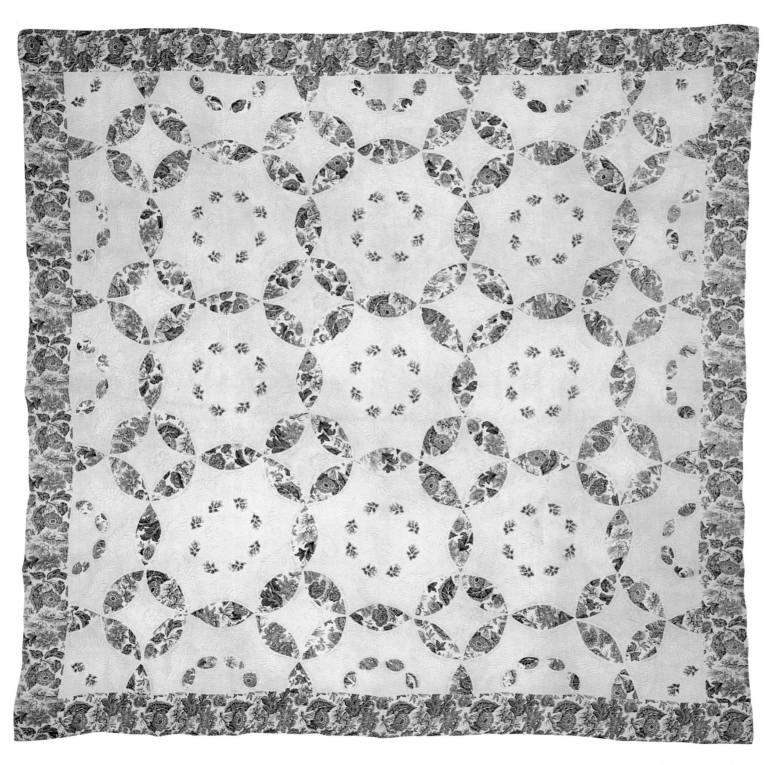

Pattern unknown, c. 1830, appliquéd cotton, quiltmaker unknown, 90" x 90". This elegant early quilt features beautiful stuffed work. The white areas are reverse appliquéd over the floral-printed fabric. Bequest of Elizabeth S. Bonham. *Collection of The York County Heritage Trust, PA.*

Pattern unknown, c. 1840, appliquéd cotton, by Mary Smith Maughlin (1797-1867), probably Airville, 83" x 81". Exquisite quilting enhances this possibly original design, with seven borders and appliqué work in the set-in corners. The opposite corners are two different appliqué patterns. *Collection of Beth Grove Wittenbrader.*

Mountain Star, c. 1930, appliquéd cotton, by Lizzie Slimmer Baile, Hanover, 87" x 69". The unusual zig zag design in the sashing makes this a unique piece. The owner of this quilt had it "squirreled away"! This appliqué design is a Mountain Mist pattern. *Collection of Catherine Baile Shaffer.*

Pattern unknown, c. 1930, pieced and appliquéd cotton, by Mary Wolgamuth Dentler, Dover Township, 74" x 61". It was all a coincidence! The day this quilt was documented, another quilt by the same maker was also being documented. Relatives were reunited through their quilts. *Collection of Patsy Elaine Drawbaugh Hartnett.*

Pattern unknown, c. 1930, pieced and appliquéd cotton, quiltmaker unknown, 78" x 78". This striking appliquéd quilt features a patriotic theme. One block is different from the others. *Collection of Joanne Henry.*

Barbara Ellen Hoffman Kunkle (1858-1930). *Collection of Gene L. and Vivian M. Hauer.*

Pattern unknown, c. 1890, appliquéd cotton, by Barbara Ellen Hoffman Kunkle, Springettsbury Township, 86" x 86". This quilt and the next demonstrate why we use the term "original design" with caution. When the first quilt came to be documented we believed we had found an original pattern. When the second quilt appeared — with the same design in a different orientation — we learned to use the term "original" very carefully. *Collection of Gene L. and Vivian M. Hauer.*

Pattern unknown, c. 1850, appliquéd cotton, possibly by (____) Berkheimer, 80" x 79". *Collection of Thelma Klinedinst.*

Nine Patch with pieced sashing, pieced cotton, c. 1890, by Eliza S. Border, Glen Rock, 83" x 70". York Countians are known for their thrift. Sometimes quilters had many little bits of the same fabric but not enough to make the whole shape they needed. They simply sewed the bits together to make a bigger piece and went right on with their patchwork. Note the stamped "Princely" motif, possibly a fabric or garment manufacturer. *Collection of Suzanne Robertson.*

Sampler, c. 1900-1930, pieced cotton, by Louise T. Manifold, Lower Chanceford Township, 82" x 82". *Collection of Jane E. Flaharty.*

The granddaughter of Louise Tabor Wiley Manifold shares that her grandmother ". . . made [quilts] out of necessity for warmth. I can remember as a child, she delivered them to our home in the fall. She placed them on the beds between a sheet blanket and a bedspread. She added a piece of material across the top to keep them from being soiled by our hands and faces. The quilts did not get dirty and therefore, did not get washed. There was no unnecessary washing of anything. What a conservative! In the spring, she came back and gathered them for storage again. She had an eye for creativity and could make almost anything out of nothing. She used old coats and worn blankets for batting. Most of the material she used was given to her or she rummaged out of scraps."

Ohio Star, pieced cotton, 1836, probably by Susan Demuth Hay, 93" x 93". *Collection of William H. Kain III.*

The stamping on the back fabric indicates the end of a run of muslin. This may have come from a mill in Rhode Island.

Susan Demuth Hay. *Collection of William H. Kain III.*

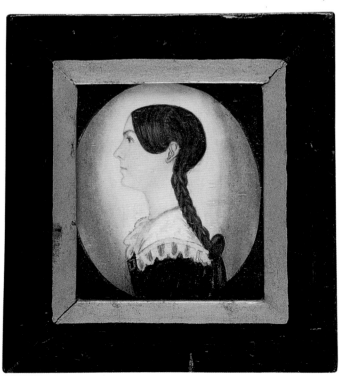

Miniature watercolor portrait of Susan Demuth Hay, 1836. *Collection of William H. Kain III.*

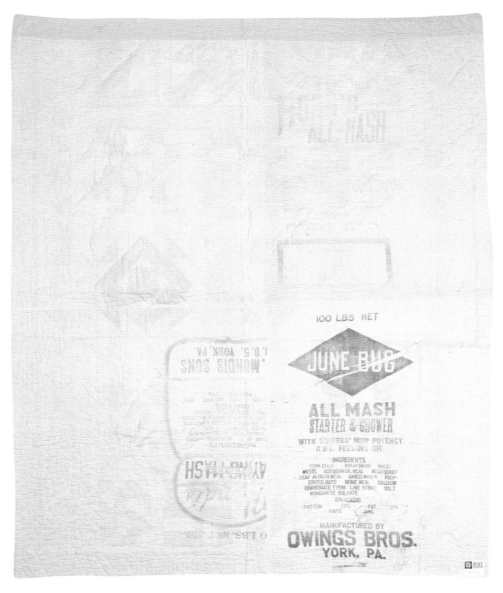

Sampler, c. 1930, pieced cotton, quiltmaker unknown, 74" x 63". This tied sampler quilt made of shirting fabrics and feed sacks is a good example of using recycled fabrics. *Private collection*.

Reverse side of sampler quilt. There is no doubt that this is a York County quilt. Note the printing on the feed sacks of the back: "Owings Bros., York, PA." and "Mundis Sons, York, PA."

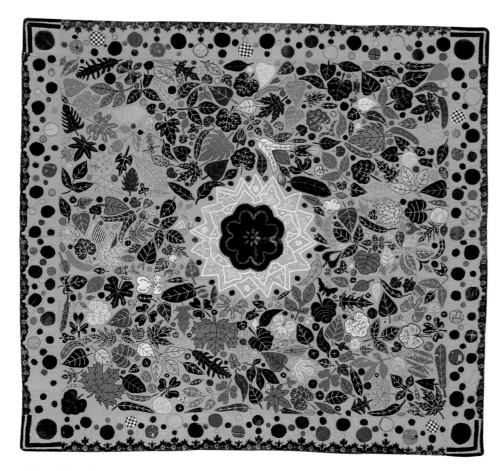

Original Leaf Appliqué, c. 1890, appliquéd assorted fabrics, by Corean Liggitt (1872-1946), Hopewell Township, 71" x 77". *Collection of Dean R. and Mina Seitz Hersey.*

Some fabrics in this quilt were recycled from a dress bustle. The center embossed motif is surrounded by intricate threadwork. Embroidery stitches were used to connect parallel narrow bands of purchased braid and purchased motifs were added to form an intricate lace-like pattern. The maker gathered leaves from her yard to use for patterns. The appliqué work was done by turning under the edges, machine topstitching, and then blanket-stitching on top of the edges. The quilt is tied with perle cotton and was given as a wedding gift to a family member in 1892. The maker is self-taught and this was her first quilt!

Reverse of Leaf Appliqué. Men's handkerchiefs printed with multi-color floral motifs were assembled for the back.

Corean Liggitt (1872-1946). *Collection of Dean R. and Mina Seitz Hersey.*

Touching Stars, c. 1890 with 1930 borders, pieced cotton, quiltmaker unknown, 69" x 71". *Private Collection.*

Mariner's Compass, c. 1830, appliquéd cotton, quiltmaker unknown, 89" x 89". This quilt is a true curiosity. When held up to a light source, one can see that the center portion, the Mariner's Compass, was appliquéd over an earlier Lone Star, leaving the original borders intact. The Mariner's Compass was then quilted through all layers. The Lone Star with the stuffed border is dated c. 1810, the Mariner's Compass c. 1830. *Collection of Deborah F. Cooney.*

Mariner's Compass/Lone Star as viewed in front of a light source.

Rose Dream, c. 1930, pieced and appliquéd cotton, by Clara Emig Brillhart, Admire, 71" x 70". *Private Collection.*

Butterflies, c. 1930, appliquéd cotton, by Emma Aldinger Harlacker, 77" x 64". *Collection of Pauline Stitely.*

Patchwork was used as the batting. The coloration and the seams can be seen through the outer fabric when held in front of a light source.

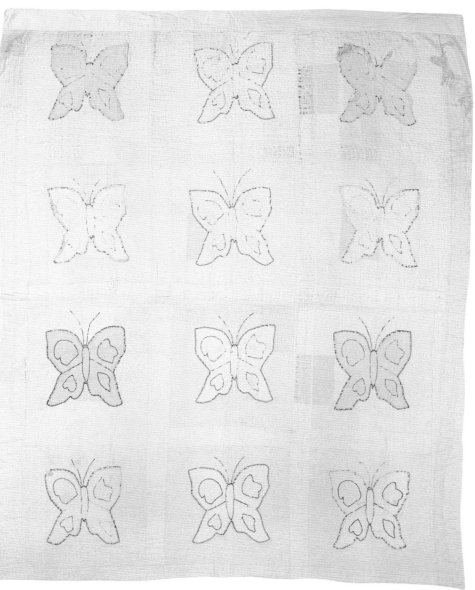

Tin quilt marker. A quiltmaker's tool for marking quilting lines, this one is an example of the popular cable pattern. *Collection of John and Wendy Buchart.*

A worn quilt was used as batting for this butterfly quilt. With a light from behind, colored patches can be seen underneath the layer of butterflies and in the border area where the top fabric has deteriorated.

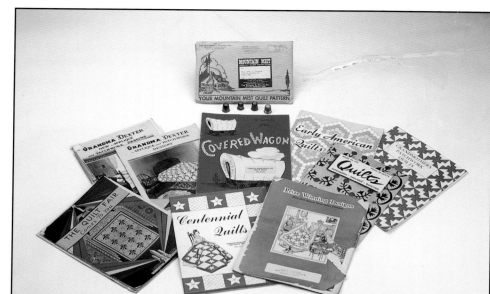

Quilt patterns and thimbles used by Elizabeth Smyser Trostle. *Collection of Mr. and Mrs. Robert Hartsough.*

Churn Dash Variation, c. 1910, pieced cotton, by Mary E. Grim, Red Lion, 81" x 76". In three of the squares we can clearly see the Churn Dash pattern. *Collection of Jeffrey Ness.*

Whirligig/Swastika, c. 1910, pieced cotton, quiltmaker unknown, 74" x 67". *Collection of Michele McClure Blevins.*

This traditional and religious symbol was tainted by its association with Nazi Germany. Known to quilters by many names, including Fly Foot, Devil's Puzzle, Indian Emblem, and Swastika, the pattern and its variations flourished for generations, but political sensitivity caused many to hide these quilts in shame. This quilt was hidden in its plain white tied wrapper. The sampler quilt on page 147 contains a Swastika block adjacent to part of a Whirligig block.

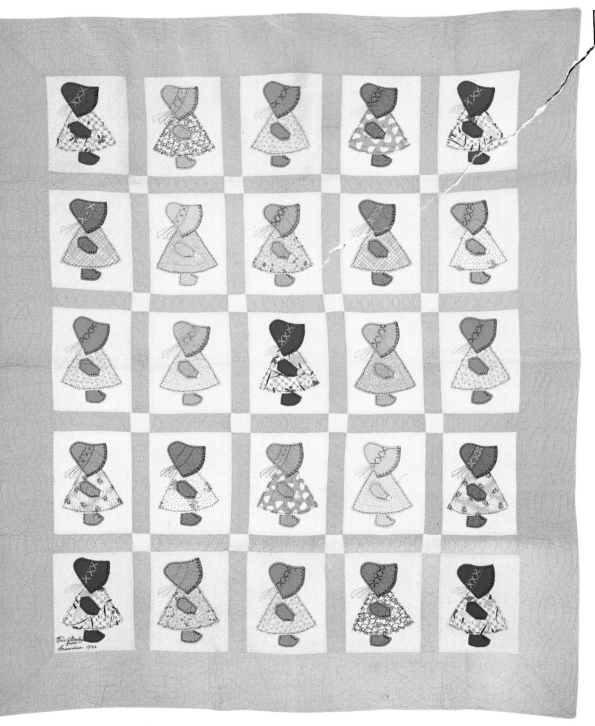

Sunbonnet Sue, 1936, pieced cotton, by Elizabeth Kerchner, Shrewsbury Township, 85" x 71". *Collection of Stanley Fourhman and Lila Fourhman-Shaull.*

When Sarah Jane Ziegler married into the Heathcote family, she married into the fabric of York County history. For nearly a century, when mills of every type dotted the county, the Heathcotes played a key role. Their mills in and around Glen Rock kept hundreds employed, some mills turning grain into food, some turning mounds of wool into miles of finished fabric.

William Heathcote began the family's history of millwork. He was born in 1806 in Cheshire, England, where he was raised near the cotton factories that churned out yardage for the world. Heathcote came to America as a young man of twenty, and for a decade, operated a woolen mill in Chester County, Pennsylvania. During that time, he married Elizabeth Van Zant. When she died two years later, William headed off to Ohio. William Heathcote would marry twice more during his life — both times to women much younger than he. In all, he would have eleven children.

On his return to Pennsylvania he settled in southern York County, opening his first mill on what is now Main Street in Glen Rock. Soon that town would be known as Heathcote Station. Yet, according to family, when the bustling locale acquired a post office, in 1843, William, inspired by the writings of Sir Walter Scott, changed the name to Glen Rock. He was involved in a host of mill ventures, including a grist mill at 50 Water Street, now known as the Glen Rock Mill Inn. He also built a factory to make woolen blankets and felt, and another to make boots and shoes. As a community leader, Heathcote donated land for the Zion Lutheran Church, and although he taught Sunday school there, he did not become a member until his later years.

Heathcote's fifth child, Lewin, narrowly missed becoming part of an infamous chapter of the Civil War as a prisoner in the Andersonville prison, where thousands of Union soldiers died in squalid conditions. Although Lewin Heathcote was captured by Confederate forces and was on his way to Andersonville, he was exchanged for rebel prisoners of war. Today, his name is listed on the Monument of Eternal Light at Gettysburg.

In 1864, Lewin married Sarah Jane Ziegler of Glen Rock. He ran his father's mill businesses, as L.K. Heathcote and Company, and as the Keystone Felt Mills. The couple settled into a home at 14 Church Street, where Sarah and her mother are reputed to have made their outstanding quilts, apparently making good use of the materials from the Heathcote mills. Family members say mill scraps are worked into several of her quilts. Sarah was also an exquisite artisan with silk, which she included in many of her works. Those silks may have come from York's active silk industry.

Sarah and Lewin's daughter Lottie Elva was a serious and highly talented musician, who became an organist at Zion Lutheran Church while she was just eleven years old. Lottie later studied at the Peabody Conservatory of Music in Baltimore, and about 1895, was planning a piano concert tour of Europe. All that changed because of a handsome young doctor from Baltimore named Jeremiah Fletcher Lutz.

J. Fletcher Lutz was born and raised in Baltimore, but every summer his mother escaped with her two sons to the clean, healthy air at the Methodist Campground Inn in New Freedom. One day, young Dr. Lutz spotted the attractive Lottie on a street in New Freedom and was immediately smitten. He said, "She was the prettiest girl I had ever seen." According to family, Dr. Lutz arranged an introduction and began courting Lottie. Not only was the object of his ardor a near professional pianist, she was also an accomplished equestrian. In his determination to win Lottie's heart, Dr. Lutz tried to take a jump with his horse, failed, and was thrown to the ground. Lutz broke a toe and wounded his pride, since Lottie had to help him home.

The couple married in September 1895. Dr. Lutz, considered a pioneer in the fledgling field of x-rays, was successful enough to extend his practice from Glen Rock, to York, to Baltimore. He became so renowned in his field of roentgenography (radiology) that his obituary in 1949 was carried in a leading medical journal. As a hobby, Lutz became a championship breeder of Great Danes who won prizes up and down the East Coast. At one time the doctor had forty dogs.

Lottie's interest in music continued throughout her life. As far as the family knows, she never pursued the quilting tradition of her mother and grandmother. However, through her care, these exquisite works were preserved for us to appreciate today. (Susan Preston Lutz, Lineage of Lutz of Baltimore, Heathcote of Glen Rock)